Major Characters in Freud's
Most Fascinating Case History

Dora

"In the first bloom of youth—a girl of intelligent and engaging looks. . . . She was clearly satisfied neither with herself nor with her family. . . . One day her parents were thrown into a state of great alarm by finding . . . a letter in which she took leave of them because, as she said, she could no longer endure her life."

Dora's Mother

"She presented the picture . . . of what might be called the 'house-wife's psychosis.' She had no understanding for her children's more active interests, and was occupied all day long in cleaning the house with its furniture and utensils and in keeping them clean—to such an extent as to make it almost impossible to use or enjoy them."

Dora's Father

"Her father was in the late forties, a man of rather unusual activity and talents, a large manufacturer in very comfortable circumstances. His daughter was most tenderly attached to him, and for that reason her critical powers, which developed early, took all the more offence at many of his actions and peculiarities."

Herr K. and his wife, Frau K.

"One day it had been decided that [Dora and her family] were to move to Vienna, and Dora began to suspect a hidden connection. And sure enough, they had scarcely been three weeks in Vienna when she heard that the K.'s had moved there as well. . . . She frequently met her father with Frau K. in the street. She also met Herr K. very often, and he always used to turn around and look after her; and once when he had met her out by herself he had followed her for a long way, so as to make sure where she was going and whether she might not have a rendezvous."

Volumes in the Collier Books Edition of
The Collected Papers of Sigmund Freud

Each volume has an introduction by the editor,
PHILIP RIEFF

DORA

An Analysis of a Case of Hysteria

SIGMUND FREUD

WITH AN INTRODUCTION BY THE EDITOR,
PHILIP RIEFF

Collier Books
Macmillan Publishing Company
New York

Collier Books
Macmillan Publishing Company
866 Third Avenue
New York, NY 10022

Macmillan Publishing Company is part of the Maxwell Communication
Group of Companies.

This Collier Books edition is published by arrangement with Basic Books, Inc.

"The Library of Congress cataloged the first issue of this title as follows:"
Freud, Sigmund, 1856–1939.
[Selections. English, 1963]
Collected papers. With an introd. by the editor, Philip Rieff.
[New York, Collier Books, 1963]
10 v. 18 cm.
Includes papers originally collected in Sammlung kleiner schriften zur
Neurosenlehre.
Cover title.
Contents: [1] The history of the psychoanalytic movement.—[2] Early psychoanalytic writings.—[3] Therapy and technique.—[4] Dora, an analysis of a case of hysteria.—[5] The sexual enlightenment of children.—[6] General psychological theory.—[7] Three case histories.—[8] Sexuality and the psychology of love.—[9] Character and culture.—[10] Studies in parapsychology.
1. Psychoanalysis I. Rieff, Philip, 1922–   ed.
BF173.F675   131.3462   63-14965
MARC
Library of Congress   [8303r83]rev2

ISBN 0-02-050987-1

Macmillan books are available at special discounts for bulk purchases for sales promotions, premiums, fund-raising, or educational use. For details, contact:

Special Sales Director
Macmillan Publishing Company
866 Third Avenue
New York, NY 10022

First Collier Books Edition 1963

First Collier Books Trade Edition 1993

10 9 8 7 6 5 4

PRINTED IN THE UNITED STATES OF AMERICA

CONTENTS

INTRODUCTION

On October 14, 1900, Freud announced to his epistolary confessor, the Berlin physician and biologist Wilhelm Fliess, that he was onto a case worth recording as history. "It has been a lively time, and I have a new patient, a girl of eighteen; the case has opened smoothly to my collection of picklocks." On January 25, 1901, another letter went off to Fliess, reporting that the case was closed, the history written; "the consequence is that today I feel short of a drug." The intoxicating effort was his history of the case of an hysterical girl, called here "Dora."

The day after he had finished the writing, Freud felt certain that this case history was "the subtlest thing I have written so far." The subtlety of it would be enough to put people off, "even more than usual," he concluded, thus showing even more than his normal suspicion of the reading public. His ambivalence toward that public rarely subsided. In this case, he had composed a specially valuable hostage to posterity, and yet, bound by ties of ego to the present, Freud worried about the way in which this case history would be received. He therefore postponed publication for years. The young lady had broken off treatment on the last day of the year 1900 (Freud sometimes had a poor memory for dates, and as late as 1933, in a footnote added to the main essay of this volume, insisted that the case had ended exactly a year earlier than in fact it did). Freud wrote the case in the month immediately following. He sent the manuscript in for publication and then quickly retrieved it, holding back until 1905. Such reluctance on the part of an ambitious author may reflect uncertainty about the quality of the work or about the adequacy of its potential audience—or both. Patently, Freud was confident about the work; it was the audience that he suspected.

If it is admitted that art and science have the power to do good, then it must also be admitted that they have the power to do harm. Moreover, the audience for a given work of art or science may receive it in a corrupt way, thus corrupting it. As there are corrupt works of art, so are there also corrupt audiences. Freud was aware of the dangers to which his work was specially vulnerable, once he let go. A case history, for example, has a cast of real characters. To reveal the ambiguous inner dynamics of outwardly blameless or pathetic lives was to risk cruel misunderstanding. Freud spends much of his preface arguing, not the merits of the case, but the merits of publishing the case. Much of the prefatory matter is thus now obsolete. In the name of truth and art, we publish everything nowadays, no matter how prurient the reader's interest or how unprepared his taste. Think how few readers there would be for, say, the most famous publications of Henry Miller if only those with serious literary interest and training constituted their readership. Nowadays, authors have markets rather than readers. In a preface to paperback editions of any of Freud's writings, it may be worth saying that there is nothing in any of them for the market, but only for readers.

Dora suffered from a confusion of inclination toward men and women. Her unconscious Lesbian tendencies were allied to a painful tangle of motives that only a master of detection like Freud could have picked apart—and yet held together in their true pattern, so that the reader can see the whole of Dora's predicament in all its irremediable complexity. The complexity is there in the subject, the life history of a human being. It was Freud's genius not to simplify and yet make clear. On the surface, the organization of this essay can be easily followed: there is an introductory résumé of the girl's life and of her symptoms—nervous coughing, chronic fatigue and other more painful, if not uncommon, miseries. Then follow two chapters concentrating on two of her dreams; and then a concluding section. Yet, just beneath this apparently simple scheme there is a labyrinth into which the narrative thread soon disappears, replaced by a mode of presentation calculated to help us see events, remote and near, simultaneously—all having their effect upon Dora. This is literary as well as analytic talent of a high order; indeed, the fusing of these two talents was necessary to the case history as Freud developed that genre. A narrative account would have distorted the psychological reality that Freud wanted to portray; no linear style, however precise, could catch the eerie convergences of cause and effect sought by Freud. The general point was made by Freud in the course of his next major case history of a woman,[1] written nearly twenty years after that of Dora: "Consecutive presentation," he writes, "is not a very adequate means of describing complicated mental processes going on in different layers of the mind." Thus the case history is, indeed, a history—but not historical in the sense familiar to readers of either the novel or any of the classic forms of written history. Precisely at this point Freud may yet alter the way in which both the novel and history will be written. We see in the "anti-*roman*," as well as in older experiments with the expression of interior consciousness (e.g., Joyce, Woolf), efforts to break beyond the narrative art form. The historians have been slower to learn from Freud; more precisely, they have learned the wrong lessons. So far as it has been influenced by Freud, the writing of history has merely added a checklist of symptoms and their social expressions to the personal factor, as a category of historical causation, instead of using Freud to open up the possibility of reorganizing the structure of historical writing on other than a linear basis.

Organized as it is, along multiple analytic perspectives, all converging upon Dora's repressed desires, the case, read as preparatory exercise in a new mode of historical writing, has a sheer brilliance which is still breath-taking. Freud pushes the protesting girl back through her inner history—of which she is largely unaware—descending ever deeper, cutting across levels of the same event, beyond the outer shell of her protective self-interpretations, to her relations with her mother, father, brother, governess, other girls, and that famous

---

[1]Cf. "The Psychogenesis of a Case of Homosexuality in a Woman," *Sexuality and the Psychology of Love*, Collier Books edition BS 192V.

couple: Herr K. and his wife. When the dazzled reader finally arrives at Frau K., he will be ready to admit, I think, that few greater pieces of detection have been written.

And yet there is no leading to a single culprit as the cause of Dora's misery: not Dora herself, nor her father, nor the man she loved, Herr K., nor the woman she loved, Frau K. Characteristically, Freud's case histories have no villains, only victims; Freud's world is populated by equally culpable innocents and sophisticates. It is the complicity of the innocents in their own unhappiness that Freud seeks to eliminate—at worst, by making that complicity sophisticated, and at best, by eliminating the complicity altogether.

What follows is the story of how Freud, the spiritual detective hired by Dora's worried father, catches up with her fugitive inner life—and, moreover, with that of her father and the others mainly involved in this group illness. The sick daughter has a sick father, who has a sick mistress, who has a sick husband, who proposes himself to the sick daughter as her lover. Dora does not want to hold hands in this charmless circle—although Freud does, at one point, indicate that she should. Her reluctance is a problem to which I shall have to return later in this essay. My point here is that all the others are also cases, so to speak, the very predicates of Dora's; and yet they are, except in minor ways, inaccessible to Freud. Moreover, Freud accepts this inaccessibility without serious theoretical question. His entire interpretation of the case—and also his efforts to reindoctrinate Dora in more tolerable attitudes toward her own sex life—depends upon his limiting the case to Dora when, in fact, from the evidence he himself presents, it is the milieu in which she is constrained to live that is ill. Here is a limit on the psychoanalytic therapy that neither Freud nor his orthodox followers have examined with the ruthless honesty appropriate to their ethic. "Milieu" therapy would involve a revolution in our culture.

Freud's own unexamined acceptance of the limits of his therapeutic effort to that of the doctor-patient relationship affected the way in which he indoctrinated his patients. That he was engaged in a work of indoctrination, which is the equivalent of interpretation, there can be no doubt. Elsewhere he speaks of having "expounded . . . a specially important part of the theory," a part touching very near the patient's own problems.[2] Interpretation involves indoctrination; the two cannot be separated in the psychoanalytic combat between therapist and patient. For the therapist is engaged in the effort to change his patient's mind by an exemplary deepening of it. In this case, Dora refused to change her mind, and suddenly quit as a final act of denial against the truth of Freud's insights.[3] This is not to say that Dora's own insights were incorrect; they were at once correct and yet untherapeutic. Freud is not interested in all truths, and certainly not in Dora's, except in so far as they block the operation of his own. Because Dora's insights are part of her illness, Freud had to hammer away at them as functions of her resistance to his insight. Her truths were not therapeutically useful ones, even in the limited sense proposed by William James, when James understands the "higher happiness" of religious believers as a check and mitigation on their "lower unhappiness."[4] Even in Jamesian terms, Dora's habits of thought had brought her no "higher happiness." Indeed, she suffered from both higher and lower unhappiness. Her intelligence and imagination had rendered her the chief victim in a cast of characters made up exclusively of victims, in one degree or another. Finally, for so destroying the moral truths with which she protected her illness, and which were components of that illness, Dora took her revenge on Freud: by ending the treatment before Freud had completed the expounding of his general theory into her particular case.

By any practical test, Freud's insight was superior to Dora's. Hers had not helped her win more than pyrrhic victories over life, while Freud's, engaged as he was in the therapeutic re-creation of her life, demonstrated its capacity to make Dora superior to some of the symptomatic expressions of her rejection of life. Her own understanding of life had in no way given her any power to change it; precisely that power to change life was Freud's test of truth. His truth was, therefore, superior to Dora's.

---

[2] Cf. *ibid.*

[3] Dora did return once more for treatment, and again, years later, sought help from a psychoanalyst. In each situation, her symptoms abated during treatment, but she remained, to the sad end of her days, a severely handicapped woman.

[4] William James' *The Varieties of Religious Experience*, Chapter II (published in Collier Books edition AS 39).

But the mystery of character never submits entirely, even to the greatest masters. There are fresh reserves of motive which, unexamined, will not yield to reason, however therapeutic might be the experience of yielding. Moreover, reason itself depends upon motives that are not themselves rational, thus limiting its strength severely at the very point of origin. Freud counted on something more than reason to achieve something more than a remission of symptoms. The *experience* of psychoanalysis was not a merely rational exercise upon fact but also a transformation of attitude. At this second level, the psychoanalytic case history crosses the barrier artificially erected between a literature of description and a literature of imagination. It matters little whether Freud's case histories are called science or art. Freud's interpretative science was itself, in practice, an art, aiming at a transformation of the life thus interpreted. All such strategies of moral interpretation—whether called art or science or religion—are characterized by their transformative function. Moreover, the decline of any science, or art, can be measured by a weakening of transformative effect. Thus do religions become neuroses; and thus, too, do psychotherapies become religions characterized by a desperate faith in themselves. We have yet to write the history of modern psychotherapy in a way that approximates the complication of motives from which it suffers.

The case history, in Freud's usage, records precisely such a complication of motive, beyond the emotional or intellectual capacity of a patient. Indeed, what distinguishes the patient from the therapist is just that capacity to handle the complexity of motive. There is, therefore, a hint of intellectual combat in this case history. When the modern detective of the soul meets his client, he must, like Sherlock Holmes, immediately exercise his mind. "Now," says Freud to the girl, almost in the words Holmes often used in first reconnoitering a case, "I should like you to pay close attention to the exact words you used." The battle of wits then begins: Freud matched against every unconscious device that this intelligent young girl can muster to protect her hard-won present level of misery from the danger of disturbance—for, under prodding, misery can grow more acute.

The tessellated quality of Freud's mind cannot be better viewed than from the vantage point of this case history. That tessellation is inseparable, of course, from the fusion of his own mind, as it confronts the experience of Dora, with his own inner experience. Freud's scientific knowledge is highly personal, an achievement first won with himself as patient. Dora ached with anger at everyone near her—including herself. Freud's task was to dismantle Dora's anger and to substitute for it that informed instinct for life to which he had himself, in his own self-analysis, won through.

The emotional combat between the therapist, experienced in the control of his suffering, and the patient, inexperienced and without the means of control, had to take an intellectual form, for Dora's was a failure to understand her true emotions. Her failure was a *willful* failure, as in all neurotic cases. But it was also a failure of intelligence, and in this "intelligent and engaging" eighteen-year-old girl both failures had to be corrected at the same time, at first by the agency of the transference, in which the girl would alter the current of her affection in such a way that Freud could gain the needed therapeutic authority; secondly, by the agency of the interpretation, in which the girl would see, in the locking of her mind with Freud's, how cruelly her own understanding had deceived her. In order to wage this private war, Freud's own intelligence had to become rather cruel at times. Dora would propose explanations of her wretchedness which Freud criticized, countering with his own; or Freud would spin out his arguments, ending with a fair challenge to his patient—"And now, what have your recollections to say to this?"

Everybody becomes indurate in the requirements of his own life. The neurotic girl hardened in her stand against Freud's interpretations; the intellectual therapist probed all the more deeply, in this case and in others where the quality of the patient was not quite so admirably suited to intellectual sparring. It was not just Dora's fine intelligence, remarked by Freud, that made disputation possible. The discursive web of treatment was spun to suit not merely this precocious girl. It characterized the method long after Freud's own stated preference for bright patients dropped out of the canon. The psychoanalyst must have something of Freud's intellectual virtuosity or he is not truly an analyst.

Virtuosity of intelligence, however, can lead into crude errors as well as refined truths. In the case of Dora, various clues indicating the nature of her neurosis implicated a certain event recorded in this case history: the girl's unresponsiveness to the sexual advances of Herr K. With irresistible brilliance, Freud followed the strings of complex motivation back to one of the painful knots in Dora's psyche, finding that, despite her refusal, Dora *wanted* to accept Herr K.'s proposition, which she understood and rejected, violently, even before he had finished making it. Dora was in love with the man she thought she detested. "We never discover a 'No' in the unconscious." Sexual distaste, like other forms of rejection, may be dishonest emotion, a defensive tactic of conscience against desire. Negation is for Freud (Bergson held a similar view) a purely "psychological" fact. A denial expresses that revision which follows the disappointment of some expectation. Dora had been disappointed by Herr K. The very words with which he began his erotic proposition had been, she knew, used before—and recently; she was not his only love. Nevertheless, because a "negative judgment" is simply the "intellectual substitute for repression," each denial makes an affirmation. A "No" from the patient confirms what the analyst has proposed. Thus, when an explanation of his "was met by Dora with a most emphatic negative," Freud could consider, rightly, that this "No"

> does no more than register the existence of a repression and [also] its severity. . . . If this "No," instead of being regarded as the expression of an impartial judgment (of which, indeed, the patient is incapable), is ignored, and if [the analytic] work is continued, the first evidence soon begins to appear that in such a case "No" signifies the desired "Yes."

By presuming the patient incapable of an impartial judgment, the therapist is empowered to disregard the patient's denials, substituting a positive feeling for the subject matter of the association. A patient says: "You may think I meant to say something insulting but I've no such intention"; or, "The woman in my dream was not my mother." From this the analyst may conclude, "So, she does mean to say something insulting; so it was his mother."

This suspicion of dislikes can sweep dislike away. We are urged to attend to all cases of vehement reproof, what people despise and what they loathe. As Georg Groddeck writes: "You will never go wrong in concluding that a man has once loved deeply whatever he hates, and loves it yet; that he once admired and still admires what he scorns, that he once greedily desired what now disgusts him." But to charge that all aversions breed from their opposites is as misleading, put thus in unexpected principle, as to accept all aversions without questioning their ancestry. Rejection is a proper activity of the superego. And the superego is not a superficial, weak thing, without its own instinctual ancestry. To uncover an acceptance beneath every rejection is to be incredulous of human goodness.

It encourages too easy a wisdom, this principled suspicion of our dislike. The ancient "Yes" to everything reigns, in the unconscious, near the sovereignty of an almost equally ancient "No," installed there by the social experience of the species. And that "No" keeps expanding its territory, at the expense of the primitive "Yes." Moral reasons may themselves have an erotic color. Dora could have turned down Herr K. for several good reasons. Perhaps, at fourteen, and with a beau nearer her own age standing in the wings, so to speak, she had not yet either the aplomb or the coarseness to relish an affair with the man who was, after all, the husband of her father's mistress. Moreover, this would have been to identify with the object of her profoundest affections, Frau K., and thus, understood even on Freud's own terms, surely an act more pathological than her refusal. Possibly, too, she did not find him quite as attractive as Freud believed. Herr K. was another counter in a most complicated quarrel between Dora and her parental generation. Freud takes Herr K. too much at face value. All he saw, conveniently, as his own interpretative powers flagged in this labyrinth of connections, was that this young female did not respond to the sexual advances of an attractive male: he had seen Herr K. and noted that he was still "prepossessing." Even supposing Herr K. quite as attractive as Freud thought, nevertheless he belonged to the older generation with which Dora was (with good reason) at war. She had become a pawn in her elders'

pathetic little end-games, her cooperation necessary in order for them
to salvage something erotic for themselves in a loveless world. The
game had gone too far; Dora refused to play. Nor, had she played,
would she have been spared her difficulties, for eroticism too is a
form of neuroticism. There was no love in Dora's parental circle;
her rejection of Herr K. was an effort, however confused and ambiva-
lent, to break out of the circle. Yet Freud's interpretation makes of
her neurosis a sort of *hubris* of distaste; the neurotic makes too
many rejections. In rare moments of libertarian sentiment Freud
arrives at such conclusions; mainly, however, he never confuses
the sovereignty of personal taste, in love or work, with the
slavery of neurotic rejection. There are no psychoanalytic for-
mulae to discriminate this difference. Every analyst must find
the line where it is drawn, finely or heavily, in the complex
patterns of acceptance and rejection which define each individual
case.

As a therapist, Freud had to suspect Dora's resentful objections
to erotic games; they had offended her too deeply. She was not
yet old enough, or defeated enough, to take what she could get,
just because it was offered. Freud ignores her youth, and the fire
of youth, however painfully it may burn inside. Dora was caught
in a charade of half-lives and half-loves: those of her father and
Frau K. She objected to being pulled into the game entirely, at
the same time that she was fascinated by it and wanted to play.
Thus, at one time, "the sharp-sighted Dora" was overcome by
the idea that she had been virtually handed over to Herr K., her
middle-aged admirer, as the price of tolerating the relations between her father and Frau K.

Of course, Freud knew that the girl was right. He had to admire
Dora's insight into this intricate and sad affair-within-an-affair. Yet
he fought back with his own intricate insights into the tangle of
her own motives; that was his error; there is the point at which
the complexity of Freudian analysis must reach out, beyond the
individual patient, to the entire tangle of motives of all the bad
actors involved in this affair—father, mistress, would-be lover,
stupid mother. Only then would the analysis have been complete,
and true, and adequately pedagogic.

Freud went far—far as time and the fatal limit of the doctor to his one patient, instead of to the complex of patients, permitted. His mind moved with breath-taking speed and accuracy. The evidence led him to know swiftly that, unknown to herself, Dora had got her libido engaged on all the possible levels: that she was at once in love with (of course) her father, the would-be seducer Herr K., and, at the deepest level, with Frau K., her father's mistress; this last Freud called "the strongest unconscious current in her mental life" because it was not in any way overt, and yet dominant. Dora expressed disbelief; she detested Frau K. Freud persists. He speaks of using facts against the patient and reports, with some show of triumph (this is no mean adversary), how he overwhelmed Dora with interpretations, pounding away at her argument, until Dora (who had already secretly made up her mind to quit) "disputed the facts no longer." Yet these facts were none of them visible; they were all of them of the highest order, taking their life from the precise truth of Freud's multiple analytic thrusts into her unconscious.

But, despite this victory, Freud still had to face the difficulty that if the patient has spun her own "sound and incontestable train of argument . . . the physician is liable to feel a moment's embarrassment." Dora was a brilliant detective, too, parrying Freud's practiced brilliance with a strength of mind that at once delighted and dismayed him. Her own interpretation of her situation was sometimes so acute that Freud could not help asking himself why his was superior.

In this earnest debate, Freud's tactic was not to dispute Dora's logic but to suspect her motives. "The patient is using thoughts of this kind, which the analysis cannot attack, for the purposes of cloaking others which are anxious to escape from criticism and from consciousness." Dora reproaches her father and Herr K. because she wishes to conceal self-reproaches. Her logic covers a deeper passion. Thus Freud bypassed the patient's insight into the rot of her human environment as part of the misleading obvious, when it was, I think, the most important single fact of the matter; he suspected her insight as an instrument of her neurosis instead of as the promise of her cure. Years later, still unable to brook disagreement, Freud was to call this tenacious and most promising of all forms of resistance—"intellectual opposition."

To relax Dora's intellectual tenacity, Freud's tactic was to insinuate a set of self-suspicions until he managed to convince her that she was too logical and reasoned too closely for her own good. Here his skepticism toward intellectual self-understanding is most apparent: let there be insight, yes; but too much too soon inhibits the creation of that therapeutic replica of the troubling situation for which the analysis strives. Prematurity of insight endangers the credulity basic to a successful resolution of the case; it is the most intractable form of resistance, because the patient cannot use such insight to relieve or control his anxieties or other symptoms as they arise. Freud made allowances for Dora's protective insights, for, as it turned out, her intellectual verve was just a mode of defense. Dora's acumen was obsessive. She could not let go of her painful interpretation of others in the net and look at herself; she persisted in her thoughts as a mode of revenge, while "a normal train of thought, however intense it may be, can be disposed of." Her exaggeration of rationality was no longer rational. This lively minded person was using her thoughts like symptoms, as articles of accusation against those she loved and hated.

For the patient, Freud advocated a balanced, flexible standard of reason; persisting too long in any train of thought resigns "omnipotence" to it. In a curiously exact way, Freud's own therapeutic habits—spinning out beautiful and complicated lines of argument—meet all the requirements of neurotic brilliance; he had, therefore, to exempt himself at least, as an analyst, from the critique of excessive ratiocination.[5] Freud saw little contradiction in his double standard of reason. He derogated conventional insight for tending to suppress unauthorized trains of thought—in sum, for harboring all sorts of discriminatory refinements that increased the burdens of conscience beyond the limits of consciousness. Reason aspired to no final solutions, and Freud is far from recommending

---

[5] The relentless beat of their "Freudian labors" upon themselves is often reported by Freud's early disciples. See, for example A. A. Brill, *Basic Principles of Psychoanalysis* (New York Doubleday and Co., 1949, p. 48). In one of his interpolations in

insight in every case. Indeed, sometimes the psychotherapeutic effort is downright inadvisable. Freud made no brief for universal psychoanalysis, and certainly not for any doctrine of rationalism. He was too much aware of the profound and irremediable irrationality of life to become a fanatic of reason. To expand the jurisdiction of consciousness did not mean that the unconscious could be conquered, or that fate and luck would abdicate their powers over our lives. No more moderate rationalist has ever challenged unreason to permanent warfare.

Two other papers on problems relating to hysteria are included in this volume, the first concentrating on the connection between fantasies and symptoms, with a final set of remarks on bisexuality, while the second is one of Freud's glistening bare outlines of the variety of ways in which hysterical illness may be interpreted, again with interesting remarks on bisexuality; both of these papers will illuminate the case history preceding.

PHILIP RIEFF
University of Pennsylvania
1962

---

his English translation of *The Psychopathology of Everyday Life*, Brill gives us some of the flavor of "the pioneer days of Freud among psychiatrists. . . . We made no scruples, for instance, of asking a man at table why he did not use his spoon in the proper way, or why he did such and such a thing in such and such a manner. It was impossible for one to show any degree of hesitation or make some abrupt pause in speaking without being at once called to account. We had to keep ourselves well in hand, ever ready and alert, for there was no telling when and where there would be an attack." Brill does not comment on the military simile. The warfare of the Freudians among themselves was not entirely for the sake of truth, I suspect. Aggression appears even among professional students of aggression.

I

Fragment of an Analysis of a
Case of Hysteria[1] (1905)

1. Prefatory Remarks

In 1895 and 1896 I put forward certain views upon the pathogene-
sis of hysterical symptoms and upon the mental processes occurring in hysteria. Since that time several years have passed. In
now proposing, therefore, to substantiate those views by giving a
detailed report of the history of a case and its treatment, I cannot
avoid making a few introductory remarks, for the purpose partly
of justifying from various points of view the step I am taking, and
partly of diminishing the expectations to which it will give rise.

  Certainly it was awkward that I was obliged to publish the
results of my inquiries without there being any possibility of other
specialists testing and checking them, particularly as those results
were of a surprising and by no means gratifying character. But it
will be scarcely less awkward now that I am beginning to bring
forward some of the material upon which my conclusions were
based and make it accessible to the judgement of the world. I shall
not escape blame by this means. Only, whereas before I was accused of giving no information about my patients, now I shall be
accused of giving information about my patients which ought not
to be given. I can only hope that in both cases the critics will be
the same, and that they will merely have shifted the pretext for

---

[1][First published in *Monatsschrift für Psychiatrie und Neurologie*, Bd. xxviii., Heft
4, 1905. Reprinted in Freud, *Sammlung kleiner Schriften*, ii., 1909.]

1

their reproaches; if so, I can resign in advance any possibility of ever removing their objections.

Even if I ignore the ill-will of narrow-minded critics such as these, the presentation of my case histories remains a problem which is hard for me to solve. The difficulties are partly of a technical kind, but are partly due to the nature of the circumstances themselves. If it is true that the causes of hysterical disorders are to be found in the intimacies of the patients' psycho-sexual life, and that hysterical symptoms are the expression of their most secret and repressed wishes, then the complete exposition of a case of hysteria is bound to involve the revelation of those intimacies and the betrayal of those secrets. It is certain that the patients would never have spoken if it had occurred to them that their admissions might possibly be put to scientific uses; and it is equally certain that to ask them themselves for leave to publish their case would be quite unavailing. In such circumstances persons of delicacy, as well as those who were merely timid, would give first place to the duty of medical discretion and would declare with regret that the matter was one upon which they could offer science no enlightenment. But in my opinion the physician has taken upon himself duties not only towards the individual patient but towards science as well; and his duties towards science mean ultimately nothing else than his duties towards the many other patients who are suffering or will some day suffer from the same disorder. Thus it becomes the physician's duty to publish what he believes he knows of the causes and structure of hysteria, and it becomes a disgraceful piece of cowardice on his part to neglect doing so, as long as he can avoid causing direct personal injury to the single patient concerned. I think I have taken every precaution to prevent my patient from suffering any such injury. I have picked out a person the scenes of whose life were laid not in Vienna but in a remote provincial town, and whose personal circumstances must therefore be practically unknown in Vienna. I have from the very beginning kept the fact of her being under my treatment such a careful secret that only one other physician—and one in whose discretion I have complete confidence—can be aware that the girl was a patient of mine. I have waited for four whole years since the end of the treatment and have postponed publication till hearing that a change has taken place in the patient's life of such a character as allows me to suppose that her own interest in the occurrences and psychological events which are to be related here may now have grown faint. Needless to say, I have allowed no name to stand which could put a non-medical reader upon the scent; and the publication of the case in a purely scientific and technical periodical should, further, afford a guarantee against unauthorized readers of this sort. I naturally cannot prevent the patient herself from being pained if her own case history should accidentally fall into her hands. But she will learn nothing from it that she does not already know; and she may ask herself who besides her could discover from it that she is the subject of this paper.

I am aware that—in this town, at least—there are many physicians who (revolting though it may seem) choose to read a case history of this kind not as a contribution to the psychopathology of neuroses, but as a *roman à clef* designed for their private delectation. I can assure readers of this species that every case history which I may have occasion to publish in the future will be secured against their perspicacity by similar guarantees of secrecy, even though this resolution is bound to put quite extraordinary restrictions upon my choice of material.

Now in this case history—the only one which I have hitherto succeeded in forcing through the limitations imposed by medical discretion and unfavourable circumstances—sexual questions will be discussed with all possible frankness, the organs and functions of sexual life will be called by their proper names, and the pure-minded reader can convince himself from my description that I have not hesitated to converse upon such subjects in such language even with a young woman. Am I, then, to defend myself upon this score as well? I will simply claim for myself the rights of the gynaecologist—or rather much more modest ones—and add that it would be the mark of a singular and perverse prurience to suppose that conversations of this kind are a good means of exciting or of gratifying sexual desires. For the rest, I feel inclined to express my opinion on this subject in a few borrowed words:

"It is deplorable to have to make room for protestations and declarations of this sort in a scientific work; but let no one reproach me on this account but rather accuse the spirit of the age, owing to which we have reached a happy state of things in which no serious book can any longer be sure of its existence."[2]

I will now describe the way in which I have overcome the technical difficulties of drawing up the report of this case history. The difficulties are very considerable when the physician has to conduct six or eight psychotherapeutic treatments of the sort in a day, and cannot make notes during the actual sitting with the patient for fear of shaking the patient's confidence and of disturbing his own view of the material under observation. Indeed, I have not yet succeeded in solving the problem of how to record for publication the history of a treatment of long duration. As regards the present case, two circumstances have come to my assistance. In the first place the treatment did not last for more than three months; and in the second place the material which elucidated the case was grouped around two dreams (one related in the middle of the treatment and one at the end). The wording of these dreams was recorded immediately after the sitting, and they thus afforded a secure point of attachment for the chain of interpretations and recollections which proceeded from them. The case history itself was only committed to writing from memory, after the treatment was at an end, but while my recollection of the case was still fresh and was heightened by my interest in its publication. Thus the record is not absolutely—phonographically—exact, but it can claim to possess a high degree of trustworthiness. Nothing of any importance has been altered in it except in several places the order in which the explanations are given; and this has been done for the sake of presenting the case in a more connected form.

I next proceed to mention more particularly what is to be found in this paper and what is not to be found in it. The title of the work was originally "Dreams and Hysteria," for it seemed to me peculiarly well-adapted for showing how dream-interpretation is woven into the history of a treatment and how it can become the

---

[2]Schmidt, *Beiträge zur indischen Erotik*, 1902. (Preface.)

means of filling in amnesias and elucidating symptoms. It was not without good reasons that in the year 1900 I gave precedence to a laborious and thorough study of dreams[3] over the publications upon the psychology of neuroses which I had in view. And incidentally I was able to judge from its reception with what an inadequate degree of comprehension such efforts are met by other specialists at the present time. In this instance there was no validity in the objection that the material upon which I had based my assertions had been withheld and that it was therefore impossible to become convinced of their truth by testing and checking them. For every one can submit his own dreams to analytic examination, and the technique of interpreting dreams may be easily learnt from the instructions and examples which I have given. I must once more insist, just as I did at that time, that a thorough investigation of the problems of dreams is an indispensable pre-requisite for any comprehension of the mental processes in hysteria and the other psychoneuroses, and that no one who wishes to shirk that preparatory labour has the smallest prospect of advancing even a few steps into this region of knowledge. Since, therefore, this case history presupposes a knowledge of the interpretation of dreams, it will seem highly unsatisfactory to any reader to whom this presupposition does not apply. Such a reader will find only bewilderment in these pages instead of the enlightenment he is in search of, and he will certainly be inclined to project the cause of his bewilderment on to the author and to pronounce his views fantastic. But in reality this bewildering character attaches to the phenomena of the neurosis itself; its presence there is only concealed by the physician's familiarity with the facts, and it comes to light again with every attempt at explaining them. It could only be completely banished if we could succeed in tracing back every single element of a neurosis to factors with which we were already familiar. But everything tends to show that, on the contrary, we shall be driven by the study of neuroses to assume the existence of many new things which will later on gradually become the subject of more certain knowledge. What is new has always aroused bewilderment and resistance.

---

[3]*Die Traumdeutung*, 1900.

Nevertheless, it would be wrong to suppose that dreams and their interpretation occupy such a prominent position in all psychoanalyses as they do in this example.

While the case history before us seems particularly favoured as regards the utilization of dreams, in other respects it has turned out poorer than I could have wished. But its shortcomings are connected with the very circumstances which have made its publication possible. As I have already said, I should not have known how to deal with the material involved in the history of a treatment which had lasted, perhaps, for a whole year. The present history, which covers only three months, could be recollected and reviewed; but its results remain incomplete in more than one respect. The treatment was not carried through to its appointed end, but was broken off at the patient's own wish when it had reached a certain point. At that time some of the problems of the case had not even been attacked and others had only been imperfectly elucidated; whereas, if the work had been continued, we should no doubt have obtained the fullest possible enlightenment upon every particular of the case. In the following pages, therefore, I can present only a fragment of an analysis.

Readers who are familiar with the technique of analysis as it was expounded in the *Studien über Hysterie* will perhaps be surprised that it should not have been possible in three months to find a complete solution at least for those of the symptoms which were taken in hand. This will become intelligible when I explain that since the date of the *Studien* psychoanalytic technique has been completely revolutionized. At that time the work of analysis started out from the symptoms, and aimed at clearing them up one after the other. Since then I have abandoned that technique, because I found it totally inadequate for dealing with the finer structure of a neurosis. I now let the patient himself choose the subject of the day's work, and in that way I start out from whatever surface his unconscious happens to be presenting to his notice at the moment. But on this plan everything that has to do with the clearing-up of a particular symptom emerges piecemeal, woven into various contexts, and distributed over widely separated periods of time. In spite of this apparent disadvantage, the new technique is far superior to the old, and indeed there can be no doubt that it is the only possible one.

In the face of the incompleteness of my analytic results, I had no choice but to follow the example of those discoverers whose good fortune it is to bring to the light of day after their long burial the priceless though mutilated relics of antiquity. I have restored what is missing, taking the best models known to me from other analyses; but like a conscientious archaeologist I have not omitted to mention in each case where the authentic parts end and my constructions begin.

There is another kind of incompleteness which I myself have intentionally introduced. I have as a rule not reproduced the process of interpretation to which the patient's associations and communications had to be subjected, but only the results of that process. Apart from the dreams, therefore, the technique of the analytic work has been revealed in only a very few places. My object in this case history was to demonstrate the intimate structure of a neurotic disorder and the determination of its symptoms; and it would have led to nothing but hopeless confusion if I had tried to complete the other task at the same time. Before the technical rules, most of which have been arrived at empirically, could be properly laid down, it would be necessary to collect material from the histories of a large number of treatments. Nevertheless, the degree of shortening produced by the omission of the technique is not to be exaggerated in this particular case. Precisely that portion of the technical work which is the most difficult never came into question with this patient; for the factor of "transference," which is discussed at the end of the case history, did not succeed in developing during the short treatment.

For a third kind of incompleteness in this report neither the patient nor the author is responsible. It is, on the contrary, obvious that a single case history, even if it were complete and open to no doubt, cannot provide an answer to all the questions arising out of the problem of hysteria. It cannot give an insight into all the types of this disorder, into all the forms of internal structure of the neurosis, into all the possible kinds of relation between the mental and the somatic which are to be found in hysteria. It is not fair to expect from a single case more than it can offer. And any one who has hitherto been unwilling to believe that a psycho-sexual aetiology holds good generally and without exception for hysteria is scarcely likely to be convinced of the fact by taking stock of a single case history. He would do better to suspend his judgement until his own work has earned him the right to be convinced.[4]

2. The Clinical Picture

In my *Traumdeutung*, published in 1900, I showed that dreams in general can be interpreted, and that after the work of interpretation has been completed they can be replaced by perfectly correctly constructed thoughts which find a recognizable position in the texture of the mind. I wish to give an example in the following pages of the only practical application of which the art of interpreting dreams seems to admit. I have already mentioned in my book[1] how it was that I came upon the problem of dreams. The problem crossed my path as I was endeavouring to cure psychoneuroses by

[4] (*Additional Note*, 1923).—The treatment described in this paper was broken off on December 31st, 1899. My account of it was written during the two weeks immediately following, but was not published until 1905. It is not to be expected that after more than twenty years of uninterrupted work I should see nothing to alter in my view of such a case and in my presentment of it; but it would obviously be absurd to bring the case history "up to date" by means of emendations and additions. In all essentials, therefore, I have left it as it was, and in the text I have merely corrected a few oversights and inaccuracies to which my excellent English translators, Mr. and Mrs. James Strachey, have directed my attention. Such critical remarks as I have thought it permissible to add I have incorporated in these additional notes: so that the reader will be justified in assuming that I still hold to the opinions expressed in the text unless he finds them contradicted in the footnotes. The problem of medical discretion which I have discussed in this preface does not touch the remaining cases contained in the original volume; three of them were published with the express assent of the patients (or rather, as regards little Hans, with that of his father), while in the fourth case (that of Schreber) the subject of the analysis was not actually a person but a book produced by him. In Dora's case the secret was kept until this year. I had long been out of touch with her, but a short while ago I heard that she had recently fallen ill again from other causes, and had confided to her physician that she had been analysed by me when she was a girl. This disclosure made it easy for my well-informed colleague to recognize her as the Dora of 1899. No fair judge of analytic therapy will make it a reproach that the three months' treatment she received at that time effected no more than the relief of her current conflict and was unable to give her protection against subsequent illnesses.

[1] *Die Traumdeutung* (1900), Seventh Edition, 1922, p. 70.

means of a particular psychotherapeutic method. For besides the other events of their mental life, my patients told me their dreams, and these dreams seemed to require insertion in the long thread of connections which spun itself out between a symptom of the disease and a pathogenic idea. At that time I learnt how to translate the language of dreams into the forms of expression of our own thought-language, which can be understood without further help. And I may add that this knowledge is essential for the psychoanalyst; for the dream is one of the roads along which consciousness can be reached by the mental material which, on account of the opposition aroused by its content, has been cut off from consciousness and repressed, and has thus become pathogenic. The dream, in short, is one of the *détours by which repression can be evaded;* it is one of the principal means employed by what is known as the indirect method of representation in the mind. The following fragment from the history of the treatment of a hysterical girl is intended to show the way in which the interpretation of dreams plays a part in the work of analysis. It will at the same time give me a first opportunity of publishing at sufficient length to prevent further misunderstanding some of my views upon the mental processes of hysteria and upon its organic determinants. I need no longer apologize on the score of length, since it is now agreed that the exacting demands which hysteria makes upon physician and investigator can be met only by the most sympathetic spirit of inquiry and not by an attitude of superiority and contempt. For,

> "Nicht Kunst und Wissenschaft allein,
> Geduld will bei dem Werke sein!"[2]

If I were to begin by giving a full and consistent case history, it would place the reader in a very different situation from that of the medical observer. The reports of the patient's relatives—in the

---

[2] ["Science will not suffice, nor Art,
But Patience, too, must play her part."
GOETHE, *Faust*, Part I.]

present case I was given one by the eighteen-year-old girl's father—usually give a very indistinct picture of the course of the illness. I begin the treatment, indeed, by asking the patient to give me the whole story of his life and illness, but even so the information I receive is never enough to let me see my way about the case. This first account may be compared to an unnavigable river whose stream is at one moment choked by masses of rock and at another divided and lost among shallows and sandbanks. I cannot help wondering how it is that the authorities can produce such smooth and exact histories in cases of hysteria. As a matter of fact the patients are incapable of giving such reports about themselves. They can, indeed, give the physician plenty of coherent information about this or that period of their lives; but it is sure to be followed by another period in which their communications run dry, leaving gaps unfilled, and riddles unanswered; and then again will come yet another period which will remain totally obscure and unilluminated by even a single piece of serviceable information. The connections—even the ostensible ones—are for the most part incoherent, and the sequence of different events is uncertain. Even during the course of their story patients will repeatedly correct a particular or a date, and then perhaps, after wavering for some time, return to their first version. The patients' inability to give an ordered history of their life in so far as it coincides with the history of their illness is not merely characteristic of the neurosis.[3] It also possesses great theoretical significance. For this inability has the following grounds. In the first place, patients consciously and intentionally keep back part of what they ought to tell—things that are perfectly well known to them—because they have not got over their feelings of timidity and shame (or discretion, where what they say concerns other people); this is the share taken by conscious

---

[3] Another physician once sent his sister to me for psychotherapeutic treatment, telling me that she had for years been treated without success for hysteria (pains and defective gait). The short account which he gave me seemed quite consistent with the diagnosis. In my first hour with the patient I got her to tell me her history herself. When the story came out perfectly clearly and connectedly in spite of the remarkable events it dealt with, I told myself that the case could not be one of hysteria, and immediately instituted a careful physical examination. This led to the diagnosis of a fairly advanced stage of tabes, which was later on treated with Hg injections (Ol. cinereum) by Professor Lang with markedly beneficial results.

disingenuousness. In the second place, part of the anamnestic knowledge, which the patients have at their disposal at other times, disappears while they are actually telling their story, but without their making any deliberate reservations: the share taken by unconscious disingenuousness. In the third place, there are invariably true amnesias—gaps in the memory into which not only old recollections but even quite recent ones have fallen—and paramnesias, formed secondarily so as to fill in those gaps.[4] When the events themselves have been kept in mind, the purpose underlying the amnesias can be fulfilled just as surely by destroying a connection, and a connection is most surely broken by altering the chronological order of events. This last function always proves to be the most vulnerable element in the stores of memory and the one which is most easily subject to repression. We meet with many recollections that are in what might be described as the first stage of repression, and these we find surrounded with doubts. At a later period the doubts would be replaced by a loss or a falsification of memory.[5]

That this state of affairs should exist in regard to the memories relating to the history of the illness is *a necessary correlate of the symptoms and one which is theoretically requisite*. In the further course of the treatment the patient supplies the facts which, though he had known them all along, had been kept back by him or had not occurred to his mind. The paramnesias prove untenable, and the gaps in his memory are filled in. It is only towards the end of the treatment that we have before us an intelligible, consistent, and unbroken case history. Whereas the practical aim of the treatment is to remove all possible symptoms and to replace them by conscious thoughts, we may regard it as a second and theoretical aim to repair all the damages to the patient's memory. These two aims are coincident. When one is reached, so is the other; and the same path leads to them both.

It follows from the nature of the facts which form the material

---

[4]Amnesias and paramnesias stand in a complementary relation to each other. When there are large gaps in the memory there will be few mistakes in it. And conversely, the latter can at a first glance completely conceal the presence of amnesias.

[5]If a patient exhibits doubts in the course of his narrative, an empirical rule teaches us to disregard such expressions of his judgement entirely. If the narrative wavers between two versions, we should incline to regard the first one as correct and the second as a product of repression.

of psychoanalysis that we are obliged to pay as much attention in our case histories to the purely human and social circumstances of our patients as to the somatic data and the symptoms of the disorder. Above all, our interest will be directed towards their family circumstances—and not only, as will be seen later, for the purpose of inquiring into their heredity.

The family circle of the eighteen-year-old girl who is the subject of this paper included, besides herself, her two parents and a brother who was one and a half years her senior. Her father was the dominating figure in this circle, owing to his intelligence and his character as much as to the circumstances of his life. It was those circumstances which provided the framework for the history of the patient's childhood and illness. At the time at which I began the girl's treatment her father was in the late forties, a man of rather unusual activity and talents, a large manufacturer in very comfortable circumstances. His daughter was most tenderly attached to him, and for that reason her critical powers, which developed early, took all the more offence at many of his actions and peculiarities.

Her affection for him was still further increased by the many severe illnesses which he had been through since her sixth year. At that time he had fallen ill with tuberculosis and the family had consequently moved to a small town in a good climate, situated in one of our southern provinces. There his lung trouble rapidly improved; but, on account of the precautions which were still considered necessary, both parents and children continued for the next ten years or so to reside chiefly in this spot, which I shall call B——. When her father's health was good, he used at times to be away, on visits to his factories. During the hottest part of the summer the family used to move to a health-resort in the hills.

When the girl was about ten years old, her father had to go through a course of treatment in a darkened room on account of a detached retina. As a result of this misfortune his vision was permanently impaired. His gravest illness occurred some two years later. It took the form of a confusional attack, followed by symptoms of paralysis and slight mental disturbances. A friend of his (who plays a part in the story with which we shall be concerned later on) persuaded him, while his condition had scarcely improved, to travel to Vienna with his physician and come to me for advice. I hesitated for some time as to whether I ought not to regard the case as one of tabo-paralysis, but I finally decided upon a diagnosis of a diffuse vascular affection; and since the patient admitted having had a specific infection before his marriage, I prescribed an energetic course of anti-luetic treatment, as a result of which all the remaining disturbances passed off. It is no doubt owing to this fortunate intervention of mine that four years later he brought his daughter, who had meanwhile grown unmistakably neurotic, and introduced her to me, and that after another two years he handed her over to me for psychotherapeutic treatment.

I had in the meantime also made the acquaintance in Vienna of a sister of his, who was a little older than himself. She gave clear evidence of a severe form of psychoneurosis without any characteristically hysterical symptoms. After a life which had been weighed down by an unhappy marriage, she died of a marasmus which made rapid advances and the symptoms of which were, as a matter of fact, never fully cleared up. An elder brother of the girl's father, whom I once happened to meet, was a hypochondriacal bachelor.

The sympathies of the girl herself, who, as I have said, became my patient at the age of eighteen, had always been with the father's side of the family, and ever since she had fallen ill she had taken as her model the aunt who has just been mentioned. There could be no doubt, too, that it was from her father's family that she had derived not only her natural gifts and her intellectual precocity but also the predisposition to her illness. I never made her mother's acquaintance. From the accounts given me by the girl and her father I was led to imagine her as an uncultivated woman and above all as a foolish one, who had concentrated all her interests upon domestic affairs, especially since her husband's illness and the estrangement to which it led. She presented the picture, in fact, of what might be called the "housewife's psychosis." She had no understanding for her children's more active interests, and was occupied all day long in cleaning the house with its furniture and utensils and in keeping them clean—to such an extent as to make it almost impossible to use or enjoy them. This condition, traces of which are to be found often enough in normal housewives, inevitably reminds one of forms of obsessional washing and other kinds of obsessional cleanliness. But such women (and this applied to the patient's mother) are entirely without insight into their illness, so that one essential characteristic of an "obsessional neurosis" is lacking. The relations between the girl and her mother had been unfriendly for years. The daughter looked down on her mother and used to criticize her mercilessly, and she had withdrawn completely from her influence.[6]

During the girl's earlier years, her only brother (her elder brother by a year and a half) had been the model which her ambitions had striven to follow. But in the last few years the relations between the brother and sister had grown more distant. The young man used to try so far as he could to keep out of the family disputes; but when he was obliged to take sides he would support his mother. So that the usual sexual attraction had drawn together the father and daughter on the one side and the mother and son on the other.

---

[6] I do not, it is true, adopt the position that heredity is the only aetiological factor in hysteria. But, on the other hand—and I say this with particular reference to some of my earlier publications ("Heredity and the Aetiology of the Neuroses," *Early Psychoanalytic Writings*, Collier Books edition BS 188V), in which I combated that view—I do not wish to give an impression of underestimating the importance of heredity in the aetiology of hysteria or of asserting that it can be dispensed with. In the case of the present patient the information I have given about her father and his brother and sister indicates a sufficiently heavy taint; and, indeed, if the view is taken that pathological conditions such as her mother's must also imply a hereditary predisposition, the patient's heredity may be regarded as a convergent one. To my mind, however, there is another factor which is of more significance in the girl's hereditary or, properly speaking, constitutional predisposition. I have mentioned that her father had contracted syphilis before his marriage. Now a *strikingly high* percentage of the patients whom I have treated psychoanalytically come of fathers who have suffered from tabes or general paralysis. In consequence of the novelty of my therapeutic method, I see only the *severest* cases, which have already been under treatment for years without any success. In accordance with the Erb-Fournier theory, tabes or general paralysis in the male parent may be regarded as evidence of an earlier luetic infection; and indeed I was able to obtain direct confirmation of such an infection in a number of cases. In the most recent discussion upon the offspring of syphilitic parents (Thirteenth International Medical Congress, held in Paris, August 2nd to 9th, 1900: papers by Finger, Tarnowsky, Jullien, etc.), I find no mention of the conclusion to which I have been driven by my experience as a neuro-pathologist—namely, that syphilis in the male parent is a very relevant factor in the aetiology of the neuropathic constitution of children.

The patient, to whom I shall in future give the name of Dora, had even at the age of eight begun to develop neurotic symptoms. She became subject at that time to chronic dyspnoea with occasional accesses during which the symptom was very much aggravated. The first onset occurred after a short expedition in the mountains and was accordingly put down to over-exertion. In the course of six months, during which she was made to rest and was carefully looked after, this condition gradually passed off. The family doctor seems to have had not a moment's hesitation in diagnosing the disorder as purely nervous and in excluding any organic cause for the dyspnoea; but he evidently considered this diagnosis compatible with the aetiology of over-exertion.[7]

The little girl went through the usual infectious diseases of childhood without suffering any permanent damage. As she herself told me—and her words were intended to convey a deeper meaning—her brother was as a rule the first to start the illness and used to have it very slightly, and she would then follow suit with a severe form of it. When she was about twelve she began to suffer from hemicranial headaches in the nature of a migraine, and from attacks of nervous coughing. At first these two symptoms always appeared together, but they became separated later on and ran different courses. The migrane grew rarer, and by the time she was sixteen she had quite got over it. But attacks of *tussis nervosa*, which had no doubt been started by a common catarrh, continued to occur over the whole period. When, at the age of eighteen, she came to me for treatment, she was again coughing in a characteristic manner. The number of these attacks could not be determined; but they lasted from three to five weeks, and on one occasion for several months. The most troublesome symptom during the first half of an attack of this kind, at all events in the last few years, used to be a complete loss of voice. The diagnosis that this was once more a nervous complaint had been established long since; but the various methods of treatment which are usual, including hydrotherapy and the local application of electricity, had produced no result. It was in such circumstances as these that the child

---

[7]The probable exciting cause of this first illness will be discussed later on.

had developed into a mature young woman of very independent judgement, who had grown accustomed to laugh at the efforts of doctors, and in the end to renounce their help entirely. Moreover, she had always been against calling in medical advice, though she had no personal objection to her family doctor. Every proposal to consult a new physician aroused her resistance, and it was only her father's authority which induced her to come to me at all.

I first saw her when she was sixteen, in the early summer. She was suffering from a cough and from hoarseness, and even at that time I proposed giving her psychological treatment. My proposal was not adopted, since the attack in question, like the others, passed off spontaneously, though it had lasted unusually long. During the winter of the next year she came and stayed in Vienna with her uncle and his daughters after the death of the aunt of whom she had been so fond. There she fell ill of a feverish disorder which was diagnosed at the time as appendicitis.[8] In the following autumn, since her father's health seemed to justify the step, the family left the health-resort of B—— for good and all. They first moved to the town where her father's factory was situated, and then, scarcely a year later, settled permanently in Vienna.

Dora was by that time in the first bloom of youth—a girl of intelligent and engaging looks. But she was a source of heavy trials for her parents. Low spirits and an alteration in her character had now become the main features of her illness. She was clearly satisfied neither with herself nor with her family; her attitude towards her father was unfriendly, and she was on very bad terms with her mother, who was bent upon drawing her into taking a share in the work of the house. She tried to avoid social intercourse, and employed herself—so far as she was allowed to by the fatigue and lack of concentration of which she complained—with attending lectures for women and with carrying on more or less serious studies. One day her parents were thrown into a state of great alarm by finding upon the girl's writing-desk, or inside it, a letter in which she took leave of them because, as she said, she could not longer endure her

---

[8]On this point see the analysis of the second dream.

life.[9] Her father, indeed, being a man of some perspicacity, guessed that the girl had no serious suicidal intentions. But he was none the less very much shaken; and when one day, after a slight passage of words between him and his daughter, she had a first attack of loss of consciousness[10]—an event which was subsequently covered by an amnesia—it was determined, in spite of her reluctance, that she should come to me for treatment.

No doubt this case history, as I have so far outlined it, does not upon the whole seem worth recording. It is merely a case of *"petite hystérie"* with the commonest of all somatic and mental symptoms: dyspnoea, *tussis nervosa,* aphonia, and possibly migraines, together with depression, hysterical unsociability, and a *taedium vitae* which was probably not entirely genuine. More interesting cases of hysteria have no doubt been published, and they have very often been more carefully described; for nothing will be found in the following pages on the subject of stigmata of cutaneous sensibility, limitation of the visual field, or similar matters. I may venture to remark, however, that all such collections of the strange and wonderful phenomena of hysteria have but slightly advanced our knowledge of a disease which still remains as great a puzzle as ever. What is wanted is precisely an elucidation of the commonest cases and of their most frequent and typical symptoms. I should have been very well satisfied if the circumstances had allowed me to give a complete elucidation of this case of *petite hystérie*. And my experiences with other patients leave me no doubt that my analytic method would have enabled me to do so.

In 1896, shortly after the appearance of my *Studien über Hysterie* (written in conjunction with Dr. J. Breuer), I asked an eminent fellow-specialist for his opinion upon the psychological theory of hysteria put forward in that work. He bluntly replied that he

---

[9]As I have already explained, the treatment of the case, and consequently my insight into the complex of events composing it, remained fragmentary. There are therefore many questions to which I have no solution to offer, or in which I can only rely upon hints and conjectures. This affair of the letter came up in the course of one of our sittings, and the girl showed signs of astonishment. "How on earth," she asked, "did they find the letter? It was shut up in my desk." But since she knew that her parents had read this draft of a farewell letter, I conclude that she had herself arranged for it to fall into their hands.

[10]The attack was, I believe, accompanied by convulsions and delirious states. But since this event was not reached by the analysis either, I have no trustworthy recollections on the subject to fall back upon.

considered it an unjustifiable generalization of conclusions which might hold good for a few cases. Since then I have seen an abundance of cases of hysteria, and I have been occupied with each case for a number of days, weeks, or years. In not a single one of them have I failed to discover the psychological determinants which were postulated in the *Studien,* namely, a psychic trauma, a conflict of affects, and—an additional factor which I brought forward in later publications—a disturbance in the sphere of sexuality. It is of course not to be expected that the patient will come to meet the physician half-way with material which has become pathogenic for the very reason of its efforts to lie concealed; nor must the inquirer rest content with the first "No" that crosses his path.[11]

In Dora's case, thanks to her father's shrewdness, which I have remarked upon more than once already, there was no need for me to look about for the points of contact between the circumstances of the patient's life and her illness, at all events in its most recent form. Her father told me that he and his family while they were at B—— had formed an intimate friendship with a married couple who had been settled there for several years. Frau K. had nursed him during his long illness, and had in that way, he said, earned a title to his undying gratitude. Herr K. had always been most kind to Dora. He had gone on walks with her when he was there, and had made her small presents; but no one had thought any harm of that. Dora had taken the greatest care of the K.'s two little

---

[11]Here is an instance of this. Another physician in Vienna, whose conviction of the unimportance of sexual factors in hysteria has probably been very much strengthened by such experiences as this, was consulted in the case of a fourteen-year-old girl who suffered from dangerous hysterical vomiting. He made up his mind to ask her the painful question whether by any chance she had ever had a love-affair with a man. "No!" answered the child, no doubt with well-affected astonishment; and then repeated to her mother in her irreverent way: "Only fancy! the old stupid asked me if I was in love!" She afterwards came to me for treatment, and proved—though not during our very first conversation, to be sure—to have been a masturbator for many years, with a considerable leucorrhoeal discharge (which had a close bearing upon her vomiting). She had finally broken herself of the habit, but was tormented in her abstinence by the most acute sense of guilt, so that she looked upon every misfortune that befell her family as a divine punishment for her transgression. Besides this, she was under the influence of the romance of an unmarried aunt, whose pregnancy (a second determinant for her vomiting) was supposed to have been happily hidden from her. The girl was looked upon as a "mere child," but she turned out to be initiated into all the essentials of sexual relations.

children, and been almost a mother to them. When Dora and her father had come to see me two years before in the summer, they had been just on their way to stop with Herr and Frau K., who were spending the summer on one of our lakes in the Alps. Dora was to have spent several weeks at the K.'s, while her father had intended to return after a few days. During that time Herr K. had been living there as well. As her father was preparing for his departure the girl had suddenly declared with the greatest determination that she was going with him, and she had in fact put her decision into effect. It was not until some days later that she had thrown any light upon her strange behaviour. She had then told her mother—intending that what she said should be passed on to her father—that Herr K. had had the audacity to make her a proposal while they were on a walk after a trip upon the lake. Herr K. had been called to account by her father and uncle on the next occasion of their meeting, but he had denied in the most emphatic terms having on his side made any advances which could have been open to such a construction. He had then proceeded to throw suspicion upon the girl, saying that he had heard from Frau K. that she took no interest in anything but sexual matters, and that she used to read Mantegazza's *Physiology of Love* and books of that sort in their house on the lake. It was most likely, he had added, that she had been over-excited by such reading and had merely "fancied" the whole scene she had described.

"I have no doubt," continued her father, "that this incident is responsible for Dora's depression and irritability and suicidal ideas. She keeps pressing me to break off relations with Herr K. and more particularly with Frau K., whom she used positively to worship formerly. But that I cannot do. For, to begin with, I myself believe that Dora's tale of the man's immoral suggestions is a phantasy that has forced its way into her mind; and besides, I am bound to Frau K. by ties of honourable friendship and I do not wish to cause her pain. The poor woman is most unhappy with her husband, of whom, by the by, I have no very high opinion. She herself has suffered a great deal with her nerves, and I am her only support. With my state of health I need scarcely assure you that there is nothing wrong in our relations. We are just two poor wretches who give one another what comfort we can by an exchange of friendly sympathy. You know already that I get nothing out of my own wife. But Dora, who inherits my obstinacy, cannot be moved from her hatred of the K.'s. She had her last attack after a conversation in which she had again pressed me to break with them. Please try and bring her to reason.''

Her father's words did not always quite tally with this pronouncement; for on other occasions he tried to put the chief blame for Dora's impossible behaviour upon her mother—whose peculiarities made the house unbearable for every one. But I had resolved from the first to suspend my judgement of the true state of affairs till I had heard the other side as well.

The experience with Herr K.—his making love to her and the insult to her honour which was involved—seems to provide in Dora's case the psychic trauma which Breuer and I declared long ago to be the indispensable prerequisite for the production of a hysterical disorder. But this new case also presents all the difficulties which have since led me to go beyond that theory,[12] besides an additional difficulty of a special kind. For, as so often happens in histories of cases of hysteria, the trauma that we know of as having occurred in the patient's past life is insufficient to explain or to determine the particular character of the symptoms; we should understand just as much or just as little of the whole business if the result of the trauma had been symptoms quite other than *tussis nervosa*, aphonia, depression, and *taedium vitae*. But there is the further consideration that some of these symptoms (the cough and the loss of voice) had been produced by the patient years before the time of the trauma, and that their earliest appearances belong

---

[12] I have gone beyond that theory, but I have not abandoned it; that is to say, I do not today consider the theory incorrect, but incomplete. All that I have abandoned is the emphasis laid upon the so-called ''hypnoid state,'' which was supposed to be occasioned in the patient by the trauma, and to be the foundation for all the psychologically abnormal events which followed. If, where a piece of joint work is in question, it is legitimate to make a subsequent division of property, I should like to take this opportunity of stating that the hypothesis of ''hypnoid states''—which many reviewers were inclined to regard as the central portion of our work—sprang entirely from the initiative of Breuer. I regard the use of such a term as superfluous and misleading, because it interrupts the continuity of the problem as to the nature of the psychological process accompanying the formation of hysterical symptoms.

to her childhood, since they occurred in her eighth year. If, therefore, the trauma theory is not to be abandoned, we must go back to her childhood and look about there for any influences or impressions which might have had an effect analogous to that of a trauma. Moreover, it deserves to be remarked that in the investigation even of cases in which the first symptoms had not already set in in childhood I have been driven to trace back the patients' life history to their earliest years.[13]

When the first difficulties of the treatment had been overcome, Dora told me of an earlier episode with Herr K., which was even better calculated to act as a sexual trauma. She was fourteen years old at the time. Herr K. had made an arrangement with her and his wife that they should meet him one afternoon at his place of business in the principal square of B—— so as to have a view of a church festival. He persuaded his wife, however, to stay at home, and sent away his clerks, so that he was alone when the girl arrived. When the time for the procession approached, he asked the girl to wait for him at the door which opened upon the staircase leading to the upper story, while he pulled down the outside shutters. He then came back, and, instead of going out by the open door, suddenly clasped the girl to him and pressed a kiss upon her lips. This was surely just the situation to call up a distinct feeling of sexual excitement in a girl of fourteen who had never before been approached. But Dora had at that moment a violent feeling of disgust, tore herself free from the man, and hurried past him to the staircase and from there to the street door. She nevertheless continued to meet Herr K. Neither of them ever mentioned the little scene; and according to her account Dora kept it a secret till her confession during the treatment. For some time afterwards, however, she avoided being alone with Herr K. The K.'s had just made plans for an expedition which was to last for some days and on which Dora was to have accompanied them. After the scene of the kiss she refused to join the party, without giving any reason.

In this scene—second in order of mention, but first in order of

---

[13] Cf. my paper, "The Aetiology of Hysteria," *Early Psychoanalytic Writings*, Collier Books edition, BS 188V.

time—the behaviour of this child of fourteen was already entirely and completely hysterical. I should without question consider a person hysterical in whom an occasion for sexual excitement elicited feelings that were preponderantly or exclusively unpleasurable; and I should do so whether or no the person were capable of producing somatic symptoms. The elucidation of the mechanism of this *reversal of affect* is one of the most important and at the same time one of the most difficult problems in the psychology of the neuroses. In my own judgement I am still some way from having achieved this end; and I may add that within the limits of the present paper I shall be able to bring forward only a part of such knowledge as I do possess.

In order to particularize Dora's case it is not enough merely to draw attention to the reversal of affect; there has also been a *displacement* of sensation. Instead of the genital sensation which would certainly have been felt by a healthy girl in such circumstances,[14] Dora was overcome by the unpleasurable feeling which is proper to the tract of mucous membrane at the entrance to the alimentary canal—that is by disgust. The stimulation of her lips by the kiss was no doubt of importance in localizing the feeling at that particular place; but I think I can also recognize another factor in operation.[15]

The disgust which Dora felt on that occasion did not become a permanent symptom, and even at the time of the treatment it was only, as it were, potentially present. She was a poor eater and confessed to some disinclination for food. On the other hand, the scene had left another consequence behind it in the shape of a sensory hallucination which occurred from time to time and even made its appearance while she was telling me her story. She declared that she could still feel upon the upper part of her body the pressure of Herr K.'s embrace. In accordance with certain rules of symptom-formation

---

[14] Our appreciation of these circumstances will be facilitated when more light has been thrown upon them.

[15] The causes of Dora's disgust at the kiss were certainly not adventitious, for in that case she could not have failed to remember and mention them. I happen to know Herr K., for he was the same person who had visited me with the patient's father, and he was still quite young and of prepossessing appearance.

which I have come to know, and at the same time taking into account certain other of the patient's peculiarities, which were otherwise inexplicable,—such as her unwillingness to walk past any man whom she saw engaged in eager or affectionate conversation with a lady,— I have formed in my own mind the following reconstruction of the scene. I believe that during the man's passionate embrace she felt not merely his kiss upon her lips but also the pressure of his erect member against her body. This perception was revolting to her; it was dismissed from her memory, repressed, and replaced by the innocent sensation of pressure upon her thorax, which in turn derived an excessive intensity from its repressed source. Once more, therefore, we find a displacement from the lower part of the body to the upper.[16] On the other hand, the obsession which she exhibited in her behaviour was formed as though it were derived from the undistorted recollection of the scene. She did not like walking past any man who she thought was in a state of sexual excitement, because she wanted to avoid seeing for a second time the somatic sign which accompanies it.

It is worth remarking that we have here three symptoms—the disgust, the sensation of pressure on the upper part of the body, and the avoidance of men engaged in affectionate conversation— all of them derived from a single experience, and that it is only by taking into account the interrelation of these three phenomena that we can understand the way in which the formation of the symptoms came about. The disgust is the symptom of repression in the erotogenic oral zone, which, as we shall hear, had been overindulged in Dora's infancy by the habit of sucking for pleasure. The pressure of the erect member probably led to an analogous change in the corresponding female organ, the clitoris; and the excitation of this second erotogenic zone was referred by a

---

[16]The occurrence of displacements of this kind has not been assumed for the purpose of this single explanation; the assumption has proved indispensable for the explanation of a large class of symptoms. Since treating Dora I have come across another instance of an embrace (this time without a kiss) causing a fright. It was a case of a young woman who had previously been devotedly fond of the man she was engaged to, but had suddenly begun to feel a coldness towards him, accompanied by severe depression, and on that account came to me for treatment. There was no difficulty in tracing the fright back to an erection on the man's part, which she had perceived but had dismissed from her consciousness.

process of displacement to the simultaneous pressure against the thorax and became fixed there. Her avoidance of men who might possibly be in a state of sexual excitement follows the mechanism of a phobia, its purpose being to safeguard her against any revival of the repressed perception.

In order to show that such a supplement to the story was possible, I questioned the patient very cautiously as to whether she knew anything of the physical signs of excitement in a man's body. Her answer, as touching the present, was "Yes," but as touching the time of the episode, "I think not." From the very beginning I took the greatest pains with this patient not to introduce her to any fresh facts in the region of sexual knowledge; and I did this, not from any conscientious motives, but because I was anxious to subject my assumptions to a rigorous test in this case. Accordingly, I did not call a thing by its name until her allusions to it had become so unambiguous that there seemed very slight risk in translating them into direct speech. Her answer was always prompt and frank: she knew about it already. But the question of *where* her knowledge came from was a riddle which her memories were unable to solve. She had forgotten the source of all her information upon this subject.[17]

If I may suppose that the scene of the kiss took place in this way, I can arrive at the following derivation for the feelings of disgust.[18] Such feelings seem originally to be a reaction to the smell (and afterwards also to the sight) of excrement. But the genitals can act as a reminder of the excremental functions; and this applies especially to the male member, for that organ performs the function of micturition as well as the sexual function. Indeed, the function of micturition is the earlier known of the two, and the only one known during the pre-sexual period. Thus it happens that disgust becomes one of the means of affective expression in the sphere of sexual life. The Early Christian Father's *"inter urinas et faeces nascimur"* clings to sexual life and cannot be detached from it in spite of every effort at ideal-

---

[17]Compare the second dream.

[18]Here, as in all similar cases, the reader must be prepared to be met not by one but by several causes—by *over-determination*.

ization. I should like, however, expressly to emphasize my opinion that the problem is not solved by the mere pointing out of this path of association. The fact that this association *can* be called up does not show that it actually *will* be called up. And indeed in normal circumstances it will not be. A knowledge of the paths does not render less necessary a knowledge of the forces which travel along them.[19]

I did not find it easy, however, to direct the patient's attention to her relations with Herr K. She declared that she had done with him. The uppermost layer of all her associations during the sittings, and everything of which she was easily conscious and of which she remembered having been conscious the day before was always connected with her father. It was quite true that she could not forgive her father for continuing his relations with Herr K. and more particularly with Frau K. But she viewed those relations in a very different light from that in which her father wished them to appear. In her mind there was no doubt that what bound her father to this young and beautiful woman was a common love-affair. Nothing that could help to confirm this view had escaped her perception, which in this connection was pitilessly sharp; *here there were no gaps to be found in her memory*. Their acquaintance with the K.'s had begun before her father's serious illness; but it had not become intimate until the young woman had officially taken on the position of nurse during that illness, while Dora's mother had kept away from the sick-room. During the first summer holidays after his recovery things had happened which must have opened every one's eyes to the true character of this "friendship." The two families had taken a suite of rooms in common at the hotel. One day Frau K. had announced that she could not keep the bedroom which she had up till then shared with one of her

---

[19]All these discussions contain much that is typical and valid for hysteria in general. The subject of erection solves some of the most interesting hysterical symptoms. The attention that women pay to the outlines of men's genitals as seen through their clothing becomes, when it has been repressed, a source of the very frequent cases of avoiding company and of dreading society.—It is scarcely possible to exaggerate the pathogenic significance of the comprehensive tie uniting the sexual and the excremental, a tie which is at the basis of a very large number of hysterical phobias.

children. A few days later Dora's father had given up his bedroom, and they had both moved into new rooms—the end rooms, which were only separated by the passage, while the rooms they had given up had not offered any such security against interruption. Later on, whenever she had reproached her father about Frau K., he had been in the habit of saying that he could not understand her hostility and that, on the contrary, his children had every reason for being grateful to Frau K. Her mother, whom she had asked for an explanation of this mysterious remark, had told her that her father had been so unhappy at that time that he had made up his mind to go into the wood and kill himself, and that Frau K., suspecting as much, had gone after him and had persuaded him by her entreaties to preserve his life for the sake of his family. Of course, Dora went on, she herself did not believe this story; no doubt the two of them had been seen together in the wood, and her father had thereupon invented this fairy tale of his suicide so as to account for their rendezvous.[20]

When they had returned to B——, her father had visited Frau K. every day at definite hours, while her husband was at his business. Everybody had talked about it and had questioned her about it pointedly. Herr K. himself had often complained bitterly to her mother, though he had spared her herself any allusions to the subject—which she seemed to attribute to the delicacy of his feelings. When they had all gone for walks together, her father and Frau K. had always known how to manage things so as to be alone with each other. There could be no doubt that she had taken money from him, for she spent more than she could possibly have afforded out of her own purse or her husband's. Dora added that her father had begun to make handsome presents to Frau K., and in order to make these less conspicuous had at the same time become especially liberal towards her mother and herself. And, while previously Frau K. had been an invalid and had even been obliged to spend months in a sanatorium for nervous disorders because she had been unable to walk, she had now become a healthy and lively woman.

Even after they had left B—— for the manufacturing town,

---

[20]This is the point of connection with her own pretence at suicide, which may thus be regarded as the expression of a longing for a love of the same kind.

these relations, already of many years' standing, had been continued. From time to time her father used to declare that he could not endure the rawness of the climate, and that he must do something for himself; he would begin to cough and complain, until suddenly he would start off to B——, and from there write the most cheerful letters home. All these illnesses had only been pretexts for seeing his friend again. Then one day it had been decided that they were to move to Vienna, and Dora began to suspect a hidden connection. And sure enough, they had scarcely been three weeks in Vienna when she heard that the K.'s had moved there as well. They were in Vienna, so she told me, at that very moment, and she frequently met her father with Frau K. in the street. She also met Herr K. very often, and he always used to turn round and look after her; and once when he had met her out by herself he had followed her for a long way, so as to make sure where she was going and whether she might not have a rendezvous.

On one occasion during the course of the treatment her father again felt worse, and went off to B—— for several weeks; and the sharp-sighted Dora had soon unearthed the fact that Frau K. had started off to the same place on a visit to her relatives there. It was at this time that Dora's criticisms of her father were the most frequent: he was insincere, he had a strain of falseness in his character, he only thought of his own enjoyment, and he had a gift for seeing things in the light which suited him best.

I could not in general dispute Dora's characterization of her father; and there was one particular respect in which it was easy to see that her reproaches were justified. When she was feeling embittered she used to be overcome by the idea that she had been handed over to Herr K. as the price of his tolerating the relations between her father and his wife; and her rage at her father's making such a use of her was visible behind her affection for him. At other times she was quite well aware that she had been guilty of exaggeration in talking like this. The two men had of course never made a formal agreement in which she was treated as an object for barter; her father in particular would have been horrified at any such suggestion. But he was one of those men who know how to evade a dilemma by falsifying their judgement upon one of the conflicting alternatives. If it had been pointed out to him that there might be danger for a growing girl in the constant and uncontrolled companionship of a man who had no satisfaction from his own wife, he would have been certain to answer that he could rely upon his daughter, that a man like K. could never be dangerous to her, and that his friend was himself incapable of such intentions, or that Dora was still a child and was treated as a child by K. But as a matter of fact things were in a position in which each of the two men avoided drawing any conclusions from the other's behaviour which would have been awkward for his own plans. It was possible for Herr K. to send Dora flowers every day for a whole year while he was in the neighbourhood, to take every opportunity of giving her valuable presents, and to spend all his spare time in her company, without her parents noticing anything in his behaviour that was characteristic of love-making.

When the patient brings forward a sound and incontestable train of argument during psychoanalytic treatment, the physician is liable to feel a moment's embarrassment, and the patient may take advantage of it by asking: "This is all perfectly correct and true, isn't it? What do you want to change in it now that I've told it you?" But it soon becomes evident that the patient uses thoughts of this kind, which the analysis cannot attack, for the purpose of cloaking others which are anxious to escape from criticism and from consciousness. A string of reproaches against other people leads one to suspect the existence of a string of self-reproaches with the same content. All that need be done is to turn back each single reproach on to the speaker himself. There is something undeniably automatic about this method of defending oneself against a self-reproach by making the same reproach against some one else. A model of it is to be found in the *tu quoque* arguments of children; if one of them is accused of being a liar, he will reply without an instant's hesitation: "You're another." A grown-up person who wanted to throw back abuse would look for some really exposed spot in his antagonist and would not lay the chief stress upon the same content being repeated. In paranoia the projection of a reproach on to another person without any alteration in its content and therefore without any consideration for reality becomes manifest as the process of delusion-formation.

Dora's reproaches against her father also had a "lining" or "backing" of self-reproaches with a corresponding content in every case, as I shall show in detail. She was right in thinking that her father did not wish to look too closely into Herr K.'s behaviour to his daughter, for fear of being disturbed in his own love-affair with Frau K. But Dora herself had done precisely the same thing. She had made herself an accomplice in the affair, and had dismissed from her mind every sign which tended to show its true character. It was not until after her adventure by the lake that her eyes were opened and that she began to apply such a severe standard to her father. During all the previous years she had given every possible assistance to her father's relations with Frau K. She would never go to see her if she thought her father was there; but, knowing that in that case the children would have been sent out, she would turn her steps in a direction where she would be sure to meet them, and would go for a walk with them. There had been some one in the house who had been anxious at an early stage to open her eyes to the nature of her father's relations with Frau K., and to induce her to take sides against her. This was her last governess, an unmarried woman, no longer young, who was well-read and of advanced views.[21] The teacher and her pupil were for a while upon excellent terms, until suddenly Dora became hostile to her and insisted upon her dismissal. So long as the governess had any influence she used it for stirring up feeling against Frau K. She explained to Dora's mother that it was incompatible with her dignity to tolerate such an intimacy between her husband and another woman; and she drew Dora's attention to all the striking features of their relations. But her efforts were vain. Dora remained devoted to Frau K. and would hear of nothing that might make her think ill of her relations with her father. On the other hand she very easily fathomed the motives by which her governess was actuated. She might be blind in one direction, but she was sharp-sighted enough in the other. She saw that the governess was

---

[21] This governess used to read every sort of book on sexual life and similar subjects, and talked to the girl about them, at the same time asking her quite frankly not to mention their conversations to her parents, as one could never tell what line they might take about them. For some time I looked upon this woman as the source of all Dora's secret knowledge, and perhaps I was not entirely wrong in this.

in love with her father. When he was there, she seemed to be quite another person: at such times she could be amusing and obliging. While the family were living in the manufacturing town and Frau K. was not on the horizon, her hostility was directed against Dora's mother, who was then her more immediate rival. Up to this point Dora bore her no ill-will. She did not become angry until she observed that she herself was a subject of complete indifference to the governess, whose pretended affection for her was really meant for her father. While her father was away from the manufacturing town the governess had no time to spare for her, would not go for walks with her, and took no interest in her studies. No sooner had her father returned from B—— than she was once more ready with every sort of service and assistance. Thereupon Dora dropped her.

The poor woman had thrown a most unwelcome light upon a part of Dora's own behaviour. What the governess had from time to time been to Dora, Dora had been to Herr K.'s children. She had been a mother to them, she had taught them, she had gone for walks with them, she had offered them a complete substitute for the slight interest which their own mother showed in them. Herr K. and his wife had often talked of getting a divorce; but it never took place, because Herr K., who was an affectionate father, would not give up either of the two children. A common interest in the children had from the first been a bond between Herr K. and Dora. Her preoccupation with his children was evidently a cloak for something else that Dora was anxious to hide from herself and from other people.

The same inference was to be drawn both from her behaviour towards the children, regarded in the light of the governess's behaviour towards herself, and from her silent acquiescence in her father's relations with Frau K.—namely, that she had all these years been in love with Herr K. When I informed her of this conclusion she did not assent to it. It is true that she at once told me that other people besides (one of her cousins, for instance—a girl who had stopped with them for some time at B——) had said to her: "Why, you're simply wild about that man!" But she herself could not be got to recollect any feelings of the kind. Later on, when the quantity of material that had come up had made it difficult for her to persist in her denial, she admitted that she might have been in love with Herr K. at B——, but declared that since the scene by the lake it had all been over.[22] In any case it was quite certain that the reproaches which she made against her father of having been deaf to the most imperative calls of duty and of having seen things in the light which was most convenient from the point of view of his own passions—these reproaches recoiled upon her own head.[23] Her other reproach against her father was that his ill-health was only a pretext and that he exploited it for his own purposes. This reproach, too, concealed a whole section of her own secret history. One day she complained of a professedly new symptom, which consisted of piercing gastric pains. "Whom are you copying now?" I asked her, and found I had hit the mark. The day before she had visited her cousins, the daughters of the aunt who had died. The younger one had become engaged, and this had given occasion to the elder one for falling ill with gastric pains, and she was to be sent off to Semmering.[24] Dora thought it was all just envy on the part of the elder sister; she always got ill when she wanted something, and what she wanted now was to be away from home so as not to have to look on at her sister's happiness.[25] But Dora's own gastric pains proclaimed the fact that she identified herself with her cousin, who, according to her, was a malingerer. Her grounds for this identification were either that she too envied the luckier girl her love, or that she saw her own story reflected in that of the elder sister who had recently had a love-affair which had ended unhappily.[26] But she had also learned from observing Frau K. what useful things illnesses could become. Herr K. spent part of the year in travelling. Whenever he came back,

---

[22] Compare the second dream.

[23] The question then arises: If Dora loved Herr K., what was the reason for her refusing him in the scene by the lake? Or at any rate, why did her refusal take such a brutal form, as though she were embittered against him? And how could a girl who was in love feel insulted by a proposal which was made in a manner neither tactless nor offensive?

[24] [A fashionable health resort in the mountains, about fifty miles south of Vienna.—*Trans.*]

[25] An event of everyday occurrence between sisters.

[26] I shall discuss later on what further conclusion I drew from these gastric pains.

he used to find his wife in bad health, although, as Dora knew, she had been quite well only the day before. Dora realized that the presence of the husband had the effect of making his wife ill, and that she was glad to be ill so as to be able to escape the conjugal duties which she so much detested. At this point in the discussion Dora suddenly brought in an allusion to her own alternations between good and bad health during the first years of her girlhood at B——; and I was thus driven to suspect that her states of health were to be regarded as depending upon something else, in the same way as Frau K.'s. (It is a rule of psychoanalytic technique that an internal connection which is still undisclosed will announce its presence by means of a contiguity—a temporal proximity—of associations; just as in writing, if "a" and "b" are put side by side, it means that the syllable "ab" is to be formed out of them.) Dora had had a very large number of attacks of coughing accompanied by loss of voice. Could it be that the presence or absence of the man she loved had had an influence upon the appearance and disappearance of the symptoms of her illness? If this were so, it must be possible to discover some coincidence or other which would betray the fact. I asked her what the average length of these attacks had been. "From three to six weeks, perhaps." How long had Herr K.'s absences lasted? "Three to six weeks, too," she was obliged to admit. Her illness was therefore a demonstration of her love for K., just as his wife's was a demonstration of her dislike. It was only necessary to suppose that she had behaved in the opposite way from Frau K., and had been ill when he was absent and well when he had come back. And this really seemed to have been so, at least during the first period of the attacks. Later on it no doubt became necessary to obscure the coincidence between her attacks of illness and the absence of the man she secretly loved, lest its regularity should betray her secret. The length of the attacks would then remain as a trace of their original significance.

I remembered that long before, while I was working at Charcot's clinic, I had seen and heard how in cases of hysterical mutism writing operated vicariously in the place of speech. Such patients were able to write more fluently, quicker, and better than others did or than they themselves had done previously. The same thing had happened with

Dora. In the first days of her attacks of aphonia "writing had always come specially easy to her." No psychological elucidation was really required for this peculiarity, which was the expression of a physiological substitutive function enforced by necessity; it was noticeable, however, that such an elucidation was easily to be found. Herr K. used to write to her at length while he was travelling and to send her picture post-cards. It used to happen that she alone was informed as to the date of his return, and that his arrival took his wife by surprise. Moreover, that a person will correspond with an absent friend whom he cannot talk to is scarcely less obvious than that if he has lost his voice he will try to make himself understood in writing. Dora's aphonia, then, allowed of the following symbolic interpretation. When the person she loved was away she gave up speaking; speech had lost its value since she could not speak to *him*. On the other hand, writing gained in importance, as being the only means of communication with the absent person.

Am I now going on to assert that in every instance in which there are periodical attacks of aphonia we are to diagnose the existence of a loved person who is at times away from the patient? Nothing could be further from my intention. The determination of Dora's symptoms is far too specific for it to be possible to expect a frequent recurrence of the same accidental aetiology. But, if so, what is the value of our elucidation of the aphonia in the present case? Have we not merely allowed ourselves to become the victims of a *jeu d'esprit?* I think not. In this connection we must recall the question which has so often been raised whether the symptoms of hysteria are of psychical or of somatic origin, or whether, if the former is granted, they are necessarily all of them psychically determined. Like so many other questions to which we find investigators returning again and again without success, this question is not adequately framed. The alternatives stated in it do not cover the real essence of the matter. As far as I can see, every hysterical symptom involves the participation of both sides. It cannot occur without the presence of a certain degree of *somatic compliance* offered by some normal or pathological process in or connected with one of the bodily organs. And it cannot occur more than once—and the capacity for repeating itself is one of the characteris-

tics of a hysterical symptom—unless it has a psychical significance, a *meaning*. The hysterical symptom does not carry this
meaning with it, but the meaning is lent to it, welded on to it, as
it were; and in every instance the meaning can be a different
one, according to the nature of the suppressed thoughts which are
struggling for expression. However, there are a number of factors
at work which tend to make less arbitrary the relations between
the unconscious thoughts and the somatic processes which are at
their disposal as a means of expression, and which tend to make
those relations approximate to a few typical forms. For therapeutic
purposes the most important determinants are those given by the
contingent psychical material; the clearing-up of the symptoms is
achieved by looking for their psychical significance. When everything that can be got rid of by psychoanalysis has been cleared
away, we are in a position to form all kinds of conjectures, which
probably meet the facts, as regards the somatic basis of the symptoms—a basis which is as a rule constitutional and organic. Thus
in Dora's case we shall not content ourselves with a psychoanalytic
interpretation of her attacks of coughing and aphonia; but we shall
also indicate the organic factor which was the source of the "somatic compliance" that enabled her to express her love for a man
who was periodically absent. And if the connection between the
symptomatic expression and the unconscious mental content should
strike us as being in this case a clever *tour de force*, we shall be
glad to hear that it succeeds in creating the same impression in
every other case and in every other instance.

I am prepared to be told at this point that there is no very great
advantage in having been taught by psychoanalysis that the clue
to the problem of hysteria is to be found not in "a peculiar instabil-
ity of the molecules of the nerves" or in a liability to "hypnoid
states"—but in a "somatic compliance." But in reply to the objection I may remark that this new view has not only to some extent
pushed the problem further back, but has also to some extent di-
minished it. We have no longer to deal with the whole problem,
but only with the portion of it involving that particular characteristic of hysteria *which differentiates it* from other psychoneuroses.
The mental events in all psychoneuroses proceed for a considerable

distance along the same lines before any question arises of the "somatic compliance" which may afford the unconscious mental processes a physical outlet. When this factor is not forthcoming, something other than a hysterical symptom will arise out of the total situation; yet it will still be something of an allied nature, a phobia, perhaps, or an obsession—in short, a mental symptom.

I now return to the reproach of malingering which Dora brought against her father. It soon became evident that this reproach corresponded to self-reproaches not only concerning her earlier states of ill-health but also concerning the present time. At such a moment the physician is usually faced by the task of guessing and filling in what the analysis offers him in the shape only of hints and allusions. I was obliged to point out to the patient that her present ill-health was just as much actuated by motives and was just as tendentious as had been Frau K.'s illness, which she had understood so well. There could be no doubt, I said, that she had an object in view which she hoped to gain by her illness. That object could be none other than to detach her father from Frau K. She had been unable to achieve this by prayers or arguments; perhaps she hoped to succeed by frightening her father (there was her farewell letter), or by awakening his pity (there were her fainting-fits); or if all this was in vain, at least she would be taking her revenge on him. She knew very well, I went on, how much he was attached to her, and that tears used to come into his eyes whenever he was asked after his daughter's health. I felt quite convinced that she would recover at once if only her father were to tell her that he had sacrificed Frau K. for the sake of her health. But, I added, I hoped he would not let himself be persuaded to do this, for then she would have learned what a powerful weapon she had in her hands, and she would certainly not fail on every future occasion to make use once more of her liability to ill-health. Yet if her father refused to give way to her, I was quite sure she would not let herself be deprived of her illness so easily.

I will pass over the details which showed how entirely correct all of this was, and I will instead add a few general remarks upon the part played in hysteria by the *motives of illness*. A *motive* for being ill is sharply to be distinguished as a concept from a *liability*

to being ill,—from the material out of which symptoms are
formed. The motives have no share in the formation of symptoms,
and indeed are not present at the beginning of the illness. They
only appear secondarily to it; but it is not until they have appeared
that the disease is fully constituted.[27] Their presence can be reck-
oned upon in every case in which there is real suffering and which
is of fairly long standing. A symptom comes into the patient's
mental life at first as an unwelcome guest; it has everything against
it; and that is why it may vanish so easily, apparently of its own
accord, under the influence of time. To begin with, there is no
use to which it can be put in the domestic economy of the mind;
but very often it succeeds in finding one secondarily. Some psychical current or other finds it convenient to make use of it, and in
that way the symptom manages to obtain a *secondary function* and
remains, as it were, anchored fast in the patient's mental life. And
so it happens that any one who tries to make him well is to his
astonishment brought up against a powerful resistance, which
teaches him that the patient's intention of getting rid of his complaint is not so entirely and completely serious as it seemed.[28] Let
us imagine a workman, a bricklayer, let us say, who has fallen
off a house and been crippled, and now earns his livelihood by
begging at the street-corner. Let us then suppose that a miracle-

---

[27] *(Additional Note,* 1923).—This is not quite right. The statement that the motives
of illness are not present at the beginning of the illness, but only appear secondarily
to it, cannot be maintained. In the very next paragraph motives for being ill are mentioned which were in existence before the outbreak of illness, and were partly responsible for that outbreak. I subsequently found a better way of meeting the facts, by
introducing a distinction between the *primary* advantage derived from the illness (the
paranosic gain) and the *secondary* one (the *epinosic* gain). The motive for being ill is,
of course, invariably the gainlng of some advantage. What follows in the later sentences
of this paragraph applies to the epinosic gain. But in every neurotic illness a paranosic
gain is also to be discerned. In the first place, falling ill involves a saving of psychical
effort; it emerges as being economically the most convenient solution when there is a
mental conflict (we speak of a "flight into illness"), even though in most cases the
ineffectiveness of such an escape becomes manifest at a later stage. This element in
the paranosic gain may be described as the *internal* or psychological one, and it is, so
to say, a constant one. But beyond this, external factors (such as in the instance given
above of the situation of a woman subjugated by her husband) may contribute motives
for falling ill; and these will constitute the *external* element in the paranosic gain.
[28] A man of letters, who, by the way, is also a physician—Arthur Schnitzler—has
expressed this piece of knowledge very correctly in his *Paracelsus.*

worker comes along and promises him to make his crooked leg straight and capable of walking. It would be unwise, I think, to look forward to seeing an expression of peculiar bliss upon the man's features. No doubt at the time of the accident he felt he was extremely unlucky, when he realized that he would never be able to do any more work and would have to starve or live upon charity. But since then the very thing which in the first instance threw him out of employment has become his source of income: he lives by his disablement. If that is taken from him he may become totally helpless. He has in the meantime forgotten his trade and lost his habits of industry; he has grown accustomed to idleness, and perhaps to drink as well.

The motives for being ill often begin to be active even in childhood. A child in its greed for love does not enjoy having to share the affection of its parents with its brothers and sisters; and it notices that the whole of their affection is lavished upon it once more whenever it arouses their anxiety by falling ill. It has now discovered a means of enticing out its parents' love, and will make use of that means as soon as it has the necessary psychical material at its disposal for producing an illness. When such a child has grown up to be a woman she may find all the demands she used to make in her childhood countered owing to her marriage with an inconsiderate husband, who may subjugate her will, mercilessly exploit her capacity for work, and lavish neither his affection nor his money upon her. In that case ill-health will be her one weapon for maintaining her position. It will procure her the care she longs for; it will force her husband to make pecuniary sacrifices for her and to show her consideration, as he would never have done while she was well; and it will compel him to treat her with solicitude if she recovers, for otherwise a relapse will threaten. Her state of ill-health will have every appearance of being objective and involuntary—the very doctor who treats her will bear witness to the fact; and for that reason she will not need to feel any conscious self-reproaches at making such successful use of a means which she had found effective in her years of childhood.

And yet illnesses of this kind are the result of intention. They are as a rule levelled at a particular person, and consequently vanish with that person's departure. The crudest and most commonplace views upon the character of hysterical disorders—such as are to be heard from uneducated relatives or nurses—are in a certain sense right. It is true that the paralysed and bed-ridden woman would spring to her feet if a fire were to break out in her room, and that the spoiled wife would forget all her sufferings if her child were to fall dangerously ill or if some catastrophe were to threaten the family circumstances. People who speak of the patients in this way are right except upon a single point: they overlook the psychological distinction between what is conscious and what is unconscious. This may be permissible where children are concerned, but with adults it is no longer possible. That is why all these asseverations that it is "only a question of willing" and all the encouragements and abuse that are addressed to the patient are of no avail. An attempt must first be made by the roundabout methods of analysis to convince the patient herself of the existence in her of an intention to be ill.

It is in combating the motives of illness that the weak point in every kind of therapeutic treatment of hysteria lies. This is quite generally true, and it applies equally to psychoanalysis. Destiny has an easier time of it in this respect: it need not concern itself either with the patient's constitution or with his pathogenic material; it has only to take away a motive for being ill, and the patient is temporarily or perhaps even permanently freed from his illness. How many fewer miraculous cures and spontaneous disappearances of symptoms should we physicians have to register in cases of hysteria, if we were more often given a sight of the human interests which the patient keeps hidden from us! In one case, some stated period of time has elapsed; in a second, consideration for some other person has ceased to operate; in a third, the situation has been fundamentally changed by some external event—and the whole disorder, which up till then had shown the greatest obstinacy, vanishes at a single blow, apparently of its own accord, but really because it has been deprived of its most powerful motive, one of the uses to which it has been put in the patient's life.

Motives that support the patient in being ill are probably to be found in all fully developed cases. But there are cases in which the motives are purely internal—such as desire for self-punish-ment, that is, penitence and remorse. It will be found much easier to solve the therapeutical problem in such cases than in those in which the illness is related to the attainment of some external aim. In Dora's case that aim was clearly to touch her father's heart and to detach him from Frau K.

None of her father's actions seemed to have embittered her so much as his readiness to consider the scene by the lake as a product of her imagination. She was almost beside herself at the idea of its being supposed that she had merely fancied something on that occasion. For a long time I was in perplexity as to what the self-reproach could be which lay behind her passionate repudiation of this explanation of the episode. It was justifiable to suspect that there was something concealed, for a reproach which misses the mark gives no lasting offence. On the other hand, I came to the conclusion that Dora's story must correspond to the facts in every respect. No sooner had she grasped Herr K.'s intention than, with-out letting him finish what he had to say, she had given him a slap in the face and hurried away. Her behaviour must have seemed as incomprehensible to the man after she had left him as to us, for he must long before have gathered from innumerable small signs that he was secure of the girl's affections. In our discussion of Dora's second dream we shall come upon the solution of this riddle as well as upon the self-reproach which we have hitherto failed to discover.

As she kept on repeating her complaints against her father with a wearisome monotony, and as at the same time her cough contin-ued, I was led to think that this symptom might have some mean-ing in connection with her father. And apart from this, the explanation of the symptom which I had hitherto obtained was far from fulfilling the requirements which I am accustomed to make of such explanations. According to a rule which I had found con-firmed over and over again by experience, though I had not yet ventured to erect it into a general principle, a symptom signifies the representation—the realization—of a phantasy with a sexual content, that is to say, it signifies a sexual situation. It would be better to say that at least *one* of the meanings of a symptom is the representation of a sexual phantasy, but that no such limitation is imposed upon the content of its other meanings. Any one who takes up psychoanalytic work will quickly discover that a symptom has more than one meaning and serves to represent several unconscious mental processes simultaneously. And I should like to add that in my estimation a single unconscious mental process or phantasy will scarcely ever suffice for the production of a symptom.

An opportunity very soon occurred for interpreting Dora's nervous cough in this way by means of an imagined sexual situation. She had once again been insisting that Frau K. only loved her father because he was *"ein vermögender Mann"* ["a man of means"]. Certain details of the way in which she expressed herself (which I pass over here, like most other purely technical parts of the analysis) led me to see that behind this phrase its opposite lay concealed, namely, that her father was *"ein unvermögender Mann"* ["a man without means"].[29] This could only be meant in a sexual sense—that her father, as a man, was without means, was impotent. Dora confirmed this interpretation from her conscious knowledge; whereupon I pointed out the contradiction she was involved in if on the one hand she continued to insist that her father's relation with Frau K. was a common love-affair, and on the other hand maintained that her father was impotent, or in other words incapable of carrying on an affair of such a kind. Her answer showed that she had no need to admit the contradiction. She knew very well, she said, that there was more than one way of obtaining sexual gratification. (The source of this piece of knowledge, however, was once more untraceable.) I questioned her further, whether she referred to the use of organs other than the genitals for the purpose of sexual intercourse, and she replied in the affirmative. I could then go on to say that in that case she must be thinking of precisely those parts of the body which in her case were in a state of imitation,—the throat and the oral cavity. To be sure, she would not hear of going so far as this in recognizing her own thoughts; and indeed, if the occurrence of the symptom was to be made possible at all, it was essential that she should

---

[29] [*"Unvermögend"* means literally "unable," and is commonly used in the sense of both "not rich" and "impotent."—*Trans.*]

not be completely clear on the subject. But the conclusion was inevitable that with her spasmodic cough, which, as is usual, was referred for its exciting cause to a tickling in her throat, she pictured to herself a scene of sexual gratification *per os* between the two people whose love-affair occupied her mind so incessantly. A very short time after she had tacitly accepted this explanation her cough vanished—which fitted in very well with my view; but I do not wish to lay too much stress upon this development, since her cough had so often before spontaneously disappeared.

This short piece of the analysis may perhaps have excited in the medical reader—apart from the scepticism to which he is entitled— feelings of astonishment and horror; and I am prepared at this point to look into these two reactions so as to discover whether they are justifiable. The astonishment is probably caused by my daring to talk about such delicate and unpleasant subjects to a young girl—or, for that matter, to any woman who is still sexually active. The horror is aroused, no doubt, by the possibility that an inexperienced girl could know about practices of such a kind and could occupy her imagination with them. I would advise recourse to moderation and reasonableness upon both points. There is no cause for indignation either in the one case or in the other. It is possible for a man to talk to girls and women upon sexual matters of every kind without doing them harm and without bringing suspicion upon himself, so long as, in the first place, he adopts a particular way of doing it, and, in the second place, can make them feel convinced that it is unavoidable. A gynaecologist, after all, under the same conditions, does not hesitate to make them submit to uncovering every possible part of their body. The best way of speaking about such things is to be dry and direct; and that is at the same time the method furthest removed from the prurience with which the same subjects are handled in "society," and to which girls and women alike are so thoroughly accustomed. I call bodily organs and processes by their technical names, and I tell these to the patient if they—the names, I mean—happen to be unknown to her. *J'appelle un chat un chat.* I have certainly heard of some persons—doctors and laymen—who are scandalized by a therapeutic method in which conversations of this sort occur, and who appear to envy either me or my patients the titillation which, according to their notions, such a method must afford. But I am too well acquainted with the respectability of these gentry to excite myself over them. I shall avoid the temptation of writing a satire upon them. But there is one thing that I will mention: often, after I have for some time treated a patient who had not at first found it easy to be open about sexual matters, I have had the satisfaction of hearing her exclaim: "Why, after all, your treatment is far more respectable than Mr. X.'s conversation!"

No one can undertake the treatment of a case of hysteria until he is convinced of the impossibility of avoiding the mention of sexual subjects, or unless he is prepared to allow himself to be convinced by experience. The right attitude is: *"pour faire une omelette il faut casser des œufs."* The patients themselves are easy to convince; and there are only too many opportunities of doing so in the course of the treatment. There is no necessity for feeling any compunction at discussing the facts of normal or abnormal sexual life with them. With the exercise of a little caution all that is done is to translate into conscious ideas what was already known in the unconscious; and, after all, the whole effectiveness of the treatment is based upon our knowledge that the affect attached to an unconscious idea operates more strongly and, since it cannot be inhibited, more injuriously than the affect attached to a conscious one. There is never any danger of corrupting an inexperienced girl. For where there is no knowledge of sexual processes even in the unconscious, no hysterical symptom will arise; and where hysteria is found there can no longer be any question of "innocence of mind" in the sense in which parents and educators use the phrase. With children of ten, of twelve, or of fourteen, with boys and girls alike, I have satisfied myself that the truth of this statement can invariably be relied upon.

As regards the second kind of emotional reaction, which is not directed against me this time, but against my patient—supposing that my view of her is correct—and which regards the perverse nature of her phantasies as horrible, I should like to say emphatically that a medical man has no business to indulge in such passionate condemnation. I may also remark in passing that it seems to me superfluous for a physician who is writing upon the aberrations of the sexual instincts to seize every opportunity of inserting into the text expressions of his personal repugnance at such revolting things. We are faced by a fact; and it is to be hoped that we shall grow accustomed to it, when we have put our own tastes on one side. We must learn to speak without indignation of what we call the sexual perversions—instances in which the sexual function has transgressed its limits in respect either to the part of the body concerned or to the sexual object chosen. The uncertainty in regard to the boundaries of what is to be called normal sexual life, when we take different races and different epochs into account, should in itself be enough to cool the zealot's ardour. We surely ought not to forget that the perversion which is the most repellent to us, the sensual love of a man for a man, was not only tolerated by a people so far our superiors in cultivation as were the Greeks, but was actually entrusted by them with important social functions. Each one of us in his own sexual life transgresses to a slight extent—now in this direction, now in that—the narrow lines imposed upon him as the standard of normality. The perversions are neither bestial nor degenerate in the emotional sense of the word. They are a development of germs all of which are contained in the undifferentiated sexual pre-disposition of the child, and which, by being suppressed or by being diverted to higher, asexual aims— by being *sublimated*—are destined to provide the energy for a great number of our cultural achievements. When, therefore, any one has *become* a gross and manifest pervert, it would be more correct to say that he has *remained* one, for he exhibits a certain stage of *inhibited development*. All psychoneurotics are persons with strongly marked perverse tendencies, which have been repressed in the course of their development and have become unconscious. Consequently their unconscious phantasies show precisely the same content as the documentarily recorded actions of perverts—even though they have not read v. Krafft-Ebing's *Psychopathia Sexualis*, to which simple-minded people attribute such a large share of the responsibility for the production of perverse tendencies. Psychoneuroses are, so to speak, the *negative* of perversions. In neurotics their sexual constitution, under which the effects of heredity are included, operates in combination with any accidental influences in their life which may disturb the development of normal sexuality. A stream of water which meets with an obstacle in the river-bed is dammed up and flows back into old channels which had formerly seemed fated to run dry. The motive forces leading to the formation of hysterical symptoms draw their strength not only from repressed normal sexuality but also from unconscious perverse activities.[30]

The less repellent of the so-called sexual perversions are very widely diffused among the whole population, as every one knows except medical writers upon the subject. Or, I should rather say, they know it too; only they take care to forget it at the moment when they take up their pens to write about it. So it is not to be wondered at that this hysterical girl of nineteen, who had heard of the occurrence of such a method of sexual intercourse (sucking at the male organ), should have developed an unconscious phantasy of this sort and should have given it expression by an irritation in her throat and by coughing. Nor would it have been very extraordinary if she had arrived at such a phantasy even without having had any enlightenment from external sources—an occurrence which I have quite certainly observed in other patients. For in her case a noteworthy fact afforded the necessary somatic prerequisite for this independent creation of a phantasy which would coincide with the practices of perverts. She remembered very well that in her childhood she had been a "suck-a-thumbs." Her father, too, recollected breaking her of the habit after it had persisted into her fourth or fifth year. Dora herself had a clear picture of a scene from her early childhood in which she was sitting on the floor in a corner sucking her left thumb and at the same time tugging with her right hand at the lobe of her brother's ear as he sat quietly beside her. Here we have an instance of the complete form of self-gratification by sucking, such as it has also been described to me by other patients, who had subsequently become anaesthetic and hysterical.

---

[30]These remarks upon the sexual perversions had been written some years before the appearance of Bloch's excellent book (*Beiträge zur Ätiologie der Psychopathia sexualis*, 1902 and 1903). See also my *Drei Abhandlungen zur Sexualtheorie*, published this year (1905).

One of these patients gave me a piece of information which sheds a clear light upon the origin of this curious habit. This young woman had never broken herself of the habit of sucking. She retained a memory of her childhood, dating back, according to her, to the first half of her second year, in which she saw herself sucking at her nurse's breast and at the same time pulling rhythmically at the lobe of her nurse's ear. No one will feel inclined to dispute, I think, that the mucous membrane of the lips and mouth is to be regarded as a primary *erotogenic zone*, since it preserves this earlier significance in the act of kissing, which is looked upon as normal. An intense activity of this erotogenic zone at an early age thus determines the subsequent presence of a somatic compliance on the part of the tract of mucous membrane which begins at the lips. Thus, at a time when the true sexual object, that is, the male organ, has already become known, circumstances may arise which once more increase the excitation of the oral zone, whose erotogenic character has, as we have seen, been retained. It then needs very little creative power to substitute the sexual object of the moment (the penis) for the original object (the nipple) or for the finger which did duty for it later on, and to place the current sexual object in the situation in which gratification was originally obtained. So we see that this excessively repulsive and perverted phantasy of sucking at a penis has the most innocent origin. It is a new version of what may be described as a prehistoric impression of sucking at the mother's or nurse's breast—an impression which has usually been revived by contact with children who are being nursed. In most instances the udder of a cow has aptly played the part of an image intermediate between a nipple and a penis.

The interpretation we have just been discussing of Dora's throat symptoms may also give rise to a further remark. It may be asked how this sexual situation imagined by her can be compatible with our other explanation of the symptoms. That explanation, it will be remembered, was to the effect that the coming and going of the symptoms reflected the presence and absence of the man she was in love with, and, as regards his wife's behaviour, expressed the following thought: "If *I* were his wife, I should love him in quite a different way; I should be ill (from longing, let us say)

when he was away, and well (from joy) when he was home
again.'' To this objection I must reply that my experience in the
clearing-up of hysterical symptoms has shown that it is not necessary for the various meanings of a symptom to be compatible with
one another, that is, to fit together into a connected whole. It is
enough that the unity should be constituted by the subject-matter
which has given rise to all the various phantasies. In the present
case, moreover, compatibility even of the first kind is not out of
the question. One of the two meanings is related more to the
cough, and the other to the aphonia and the periodicity of the
disorder. A closer analysis would probably have disclosed a far
greater number of mental elements in relation to the details of the
illness. We have already learnt that a single symptom corresponds
quite regularly to several meanings *simultaneously*. We may now
add that it can express several meanings *in succession*. In the
course of years a symptom can change its meaning or its chief
meaning, or the leading rôle can pass from one meaning to another. It is as though there were a conservative trait in the character
of the neurosis which ensures that a symptom that has once been
formed shall if possible be retained, even though the unconscious
thought to which it gave expression has lost its meaning. But there
is no difficulty in explaining this tendency towards the retention
of a symptom upon a mechanical basis. The production of a symptom of this kind is so difficult, the translation of a purely psychical
excitation into physical terms—the process which I have called
conversion—depends on the concurrence of so many favourable
conditions, the somatic compliance necessary for conversion is so
seldom forthcoming, that an impulsion towards the discharge of
an unconscious excitation will so far as possible make use of any
channel for discharge which may already be in existence. It appears to be far more difficult to create a fresh conversion than to
form paths of association between a new thought which is in need
of discharge and the old one which is no longer in need of it. The
current flows along these paths from the new source of excitation
to the old point of discharge—pouring into the symptom, in the
words of the Gospel, like new wine into an old bottle. These
remarks would make it seem that the somatic side of a hysterical

symptom is the more stable of the two and the harder to replace, while the psychical side is a variable element for which a substitute can more easily be found. Yet we should not try to infer anything from this comparison as regards the relative importance of the two elements. From the point of view of mental therapeutics the mental side must always be the more significant.

Dora's incessant repetition of the same thoughts about her father's relations with Frau K. made it possible to derive still further important material from the analysis.

A train of thought such as this may be described as exaggerated, or better *reinforced*, or "supervalent," in Wernicke's sense of the word. It shows its pathological character, in spite of its apparently reasonable content, by the single peculiarity that no amount of conscious and voluntary effort of thought on the patient's part is able to dissipate or remove it. A normal train of thought, however intense it may be, can eventually be disposed of. Dora felt quite rightly that her thoughts about her father required to be judged in a special way. "I can think of nothing else," she complained again and again. "I know my brother says we children have no right to criticize this behaviour of father's. He declares that we ought not to trouble ourselves about it, and ought even to be glad, perhaps, that he has found a woman he can love, since mother understands him so little. I can quite see that, and I should like to think the same as my brother, but I can't. I can't forgive him for it."[31]

Now what is one to do in the face of a supervalent thought like this, after one has heard what its conscious grounds are and listened to the ineffectual protests made against it? Reflection will suggest that *this exaggerated train of thought must owe its reinforcement to the unconscious.* It cannot be resolved by any effort of thought, either because it itself reaches with its root down into unconscious, repressed material, or because another unconscious thought lies concealed behind it. In the latter case, the concealed thought is usually the direct contrary of the supervalent one. Contrary thoughts are always closely connected with each other and are

[31]A supervalent thought of this kind is often the only symptom, beyond deep depression, of a pathological condition which is usually described as "melancholia," but which can be cleared up by psychoanalysis like a hysteria.

often paired off in such a way that *the one thought is exaggeratedly conscious while its counterpart is repressed and unconscious*. This relation between the two thoughts is an effect of the process of repression. For repression is often achieved by means of an excessive reinforcement of the thought contrary to the one which is to be repressed. This process I call *reactive reinforcement*, and the thought which asserts itself exaggeratedly in consciousness and (in the same way as a prejudice) cannot be removed I call a *reactive thought*. The two thoughts then act towards each other much like the two needles of an astatic galvanometer. The reactive thought keeps the objectionable one under repression by means of a certain surplusage of intensity; but for that reason it itself is "damped" and proof against conscious efforts of thought. So that the way to deprive the exaggerated thought of its reinforcement is by bringing its repressed contrary into consciousness.

We must also be prepared to meet with instances in which the supervalency of a thought is due not to the presence of one only of these two causes but to a concurrence of both of them. Other complications, too, may arise, but they can easily be fitted into the general scheme.

Let us now apply our theory to the instance provided by Dora's case. We will begin with the first hypothesis, namely, that her preoccupation with her father's relations to Frau K. owed its obsessive character to the fact that its root was unknown to her and lay in the unconscious. It is not difficult to divine the nature of that root from her circumstances and her conduct. Her behaviour obviously went far beyond what would have been appropriate to filial concern. She felt and acted more like a jealous wife—in a way which would have been comprehensible in her mother. By her ultimatum to her father ("either her or me"), by the scenes she used to make, by the suicidal intentions she allowed to transpire,— by all this she was clearly putting herself in her mother's place. If we have rightly guessed the nature of the imaginary sexual situation which underlay her cough, in that phantasy she must have been putting herself in Frau K.'s place. She was therefore identifying herself both with the woman her father had once loved and with the woman he loved now. The inference is obvious that her affection for her father was a much stronger one than she knew or than she would have cared to admit: in fact, that she was in love with him.

I have learnt to look upon unconscious love relations like this (which may be recognized by their abnormal consequences)—between a father and a daughter, or between a mother and a son—as a revival of germs of feeling in infancy. I have shown at length elsewhere[32] at what an early age sexual attraction makes itself felt between parents and children, and I have explained that the myth of Oedipus is probably to be regarded as a poetical rendering of what is typical in these relations. Distinct traces are probably to be found in most people of an early partiality of this kind—on the part of a daughter for her father, or on the part of a son for his mother; but it must be assumed to be more intense from the very first in the case of those children whose constitution marks them down for a neurosis, who develop prematurely and have a craving for love. At this point certain other influences, which need not be discussed here, come into play, and lead to a fixation of this rudimentary feeling of love or to a reinforcement of it; so that it turns into something (either while the child is still young or not until it has reached the age of puberty) which must be put on a par with a sexual inclination and which, like the latter, has the forces of the libido at its command.[33] The external circumstances of our patient were by no means unfavourable to such an assumption. The nature of her disposition had always drawn her towards her father, and his numerous illnesses were bound to have increased her affection for him. In many of these illnesses he would allow no one but her to discharge the lighter duties of nursing. He had been so proud of the early growth of her intelligence that he had made her his confidante while she was still a child. It was really she and not her mother whom Frau K.'s appearance had driven out of more than one position.

When I told Dora that I could not avoid supposing that her affection for her father must at a very early moment have amounted

---

[32] In my *Traumdeutung* (1900), Seventh Edition, p. 181, and the Third of my *Drei Abhandlungen zur Sexualtheorie* (1905).

[33] The decisive factor in this connection is no doubt the early appearance of truegenital sensations, either spontaneously or as a result of seduction or masturbation.

to her being completely in love with him, she of course gave me her usual reply: "I don't remember that." But she immediately went on to tell me something analogous about a seven-year-old girl who was her cousin (on her mother's side) and in whom she often thought she saw a kind of reflection of her own childhood. This little girl had (not for the first time) been the witness of a heated dispute between her parents, and, when Dora happened to come in on a visit soon afterwards, whispered in her ear: "You can't think how I hate that person!" (pointing to her mother), "and when she's dead I shall marry papa." I am in the habit of regarding associations such as this, which bring forward something that agrees with the content of an assertion of mine, as a confirmation from the unconscious of what I have said. No other kind of "Yes" can be extracted from the unconscious; there is no such thing at all as an unconscious "No."[34]

For years on end she had given no expression to this passion for her father. On the contrary, she had for a long time been on the closest terms with the woman who had supplanted her with her father, and she had actually, as we know from her self-reproaches, facilitated this woman's relations with her father. Her own love for her father had therefore been recently revived; and, if so, the question arises to what end this had happened. Clearly as a reactive symptom, so as to suppress something else—something, that is, that still exercised power in the unconscious. Considering how things stood, I could not help supposing in the first instance that what was suppressed was her love of Herr K. I could not avoid the assumption that she was still in love with him but that, for unknown reasons, since the scene by the lake her love had aroused in her violent feelings of opposition, and that the girl had brought forward and reinforced her old affection for her father in order to avoid any further necessity for paying conscious attention to the love which she had felt in the first years of her girlhood and which had now become

---

[34](*Additional Note*, 1923).—There is another very remarkable and entirely trust-worthy form of confirmation from the unconscious, which I had not recognized at the time this was written: namely, an exclamation on the part of the patient of "I didn't think that," or "I didn't think of that." This can be translated point-blank into: "Yes, I was unconscious of that."

painful to her. In this way I gained an insight into a conflict which was well calculated to unhinge the girl's mind. On the one hand she was filled with regret at having rejected the man's proposal, and with longing for his company and all the little signs of his affection; while on the other hand these feelings of tenderness and longing were combated by powerful forces, amongst which her pride was one of the most obvious. Thus she had succeeded in persuading herself that she had done with Herr K.—that was the advantage she derived from this typical process of repression; and yet she was obliged to summon up her infantile affection for her father and to exaggerate it, in order to protect herself against the feelings of love which were constantly pressing forward into consciousness. The further fact that she was almost incessantly a prey to the most embittered jealousy seemed to admit of still another determination.[35]

My expectations were by no means disappointed when this explanation of mine was met by Dora with a most emphatic negative. The "No" uttered by a patient after a repressed thought has been presented to his conscious perception for the first time does no more than register the existence of a repression and its severity; it acts, as it were, as a gauge of the repression's strength. If this "No," instead of being regarded as the expression of an impartial judgement (of which, indeed, the patient is incapable), is ignored, and if work is continued, the first evidence soon begins to appear that in such a case "No" signifies the desired "Yes." Dora admitted that she found it impossible to be as angry with Herr K. as he had deserved. She told me that one day she had met Herr K. in the street while she was walking with a cousin of hers who did not know him. The other girl had exclaimed all at once: "Why, Dora, what's wrong with you? You've gone as white as a sheet!" She herself had felt nothing of this change of colour; but I explained to her that the expression of emotion and the play of features obey the unconscious rather than the conscious, and are a means of betraying the former.[36] Another time Dora came to me in the worst of tempers after having been uniformly cheerful for

---

[35]We shall come upon this later on.
[36]Compare the lines:

several days. She could give no explanation of this. She felt so contrary to-day, she said: it was her uncle's birthday, and she could not bring herself to congratulate him, she did not know why. My powers of interpretation had run dry that day; I let her go on talking, and she suddenly recollected that it was Herr K.'s birthday too—a fact which I did not neglect to use against her. And it was then no longer hard to explain why the handsome presents she had had on her own birthday a few days before had given her no pleasure. One gift was missing, and that was Herr K.'s, the gift which had plainly once been the most prized of all.

Nevertheless Dora persisted in denying my contention for some time longer, until, towards the end of the analysis, the conclusive proof of its correctness came to light.

I must now turn to consider a further complication, to which I should certainly give no space if I were a man of letters engaged upon the creation of a mental state like this for a short story, instead of being a medical man engaged upon its dissection. The element to which I must now allude can only serve to obscure and efface the outlines of the fine poetic conflict which we have been able to ascribe to Dora. This element would rightly fall a sacrifice to the censorship of a writer, for he, after all, simplifies and abstracts when he appears in the character of a psychologist. But in the world of reality, which I am trying to depict here, a complication of motives, an accumulation and conjunction of mental activities—in a word, overdetermination—is the rule. For behind Dora's supervalent train of thought which was concerned with her father's relations with Frau K. there lay concealed a feeling of jealousy which had that lady as its *object*—a feeling, that is, which could only be based upon an affection on Dora's part for one of her own sex. It has long been known and often been pointed out that at the age of puberty boys and girls show clear signs, even in normal cases, of the existence of an affection for people of their own sex. A romantic and sentimental friendship with one of her school-friends, accompanied by

---

"Ruhig mag ich euch erscheinen,
   Ruhig gehen sehn."
["Quiet can I watch thy coming,
   Quiet watch thee go."

SCHILLER, "Ritter Toggenburg."]

vows, kisses, promises of eternal correspondence, and all the sensibility of jealousy, is the common precursor of a girl's first serious passion for a man. Thenceforward, in favourable circumstances, the homosexual current of feeling often runs completely dry. But if a girl is not happy in her love for a man, the current is often set flowing again by the libido in later years and is increased up to a greater or lesser degree of intensity. If this much can be established without difficulty of healthy persons, and if we take into account what has already been said upon the fuller development in neurotics of the normal germs of perversion, we shall expect to find in these latter too a fairly strong homosexual predisposition. It must, indeed, be so; for I have never yet come through a single psychoanalysis of a man or a woman without having to take into account a very considerable current of homosexuality. When, in a hysterical woman or girl, the sexual libido which is directed towards men has been energetically suppressed, it will regularly be found that the libido which is directed towards women has become vicariously reinforced and even to some extent conscious.

I shall not in this place go any further into this important subject, which is especially indispensable to an understanding of hysteria in men, because Dora's analysis came to an end before it could throw any light upon this side of her mental life. But I should like to recall the governess, whom I have already mentioned, and with whom Dora had at first enjoyed the closest interchange of thought, until she discovered that she was being admired and fondly treated not for her own sake but for her father's; whereupon she had obliged the governess to leave. She used also to dwell with noticeable frequency and a peculiar emphasis upon the story of another estrangement which appeared inexplicable even to herself. She had always been on particularly good terms with the younger of her two cousins—the girl who had later on become engaged—and had shared all sorts of secrets with her. When, for the first time after Dora had broken off her stay by the lake, her father was going back to B——, she had naturally refused to go with him. This cousin had then been asked to travel with him instead, and she had accepted the invitation. From that time forward Dora had felt a coldness towards her, and she herself was surprised to find how indifferent she had become, although, as she admitted, she had very little ground for complaint against her. These instances of sensitiveness led me to inquire what her relations with Frau K. had been up till the time of the breach. I then found that the young woman and the scarcely grown girl had lived for years on a footing of the closest intimacy. When Dora stayed with the K.'s she used to share a bedroom with Frau K., and the husband used to be quartered elsewhere. She had been the wife's confidante and adviser in all the difficulties of her married life. There was nothing they had not talked about. Medea had been quite content that Creusa should make friends with her two children; and she certainly did nothing to interfere with the relations between the girl and the children's father. How Dora managed to fall in love with the man about whom her beloved friend had so many bad things to say is an interesting psychological problem. We shall not be far from solving it when we realize that thoughts in the unconscious live very comfortably side by side, and even contraries get on together without disputes—a state of things which persists often enough even in the conscious.

When Dora talked about Frau K., she used to praise her "adorable white body" in accents more appropriate to a lover than to a defeated rival. Another time she told me, more in sorrow than in anger, that she was convinced the presents her father had brought her had been chosen by Frau K., for she recognized her taste. Another time, again, she pointed out that, evidently through the agency of Frau K., she had been given a present of some jewellery which was exactly like some that she had seen in Frau K.'s possession and had wished for aloud at the time. Indeed, I can say in general that I never heard her speak a harsh or angry word against the lady, although from the point of view of her supervalent thought she should have regarded her as the prime author of her misfortunes. She seemed to behave inconsequently; but her apparent inconsequence was precisely the manifestation of a complicating current of feeling. For how had this woman to whom Dora was so enthusiastically devoted behaved to her? After Dora had brought forward her accusation against Herr K., and her father had written to him demanding an explanation, Herr K. had replied in the first instance by protesting sentiments of the highest esteem for her and by proposing that he should come to the manufacturing town to clear up every misunderstanding. A few weeks later, when her father spoke to him at B——, there was no longer any question of esteem. On the contrary, Herr K. spoke of her with disparagement, and produced as his trump card the reflection that no girl who read such books and was interested in such things could have any title to a man's respect. Frau K., therefore, had betrayed her and had calumniated her; for it had only been with her that she had read Mantegazza and discussed forbidden topics. It was a repetition of what had happened with the governess: Frau K. had not loved her for her own sake but on account of her father. Frau K. had sacrificed her without a moment's hesitation so that her relations with her father might not be disturbed. This mortification touched her, perhaps, more nearly and had a greater pathogenic effect than the other one, which she tried to use as a screen for it,—the fact that she had been sacrificed by her father. Did not the obstinacy with which she retained the particular amnesia concerning the sources of her forbidden knowledge point directly to the great emotional importance for her of the accusation against her upon that score, and consequently to her betrayal by her friend?

I believe, therefore, that I am not mistaken in supposing that Dora's supervalent train of thought, which was concerned with her father's relations with Frau K., was designed not only for the purpose of suppressing her love for Herr K., which had once been conscious, but also to conceal her love for Frau K., which was in a deeper sense unconscious. The train of thought was directly contrary to the latter current of feeling. She told herself incessantly that her father had sacrificed her to this woman, and made noisy demonstrations to show that she grudged her the possession of her father; and in this way she concealed from herself the contrary fact, which was that she grudged her father Frau K.'s love, and had not forgiven the woman she loved for the disillusionment she had been caused by her betrayal. The jealous emotions of a woman were linked in the unconscious with a jealousy such as might have been felt by a man. These masculine or, more properly speaking, *gynaecophilic* currents of feeling are to be regarded as typical of the unconscious erotic life of hysterical girls.

3. The First Dream

Just at a moment when there was a prospect that the material that was coming up for analysis would throw light upon an obscure point in Dora's childhood, she reported that a few nights earlier she had once again had a dream which she had already dreamt in exactly the same way on many previous occasions. A periodically recurrent dream was by its very nature particularly well calculated to arouse my curiosity; and in any case it was justifiable in the interests of the treatment to consider the way in which the dream worked into the analysis as a whole. I therefore determined to make an especially careful investigation of it.

Here is the dream as related by Dora: *"A house was on fire.*[1] *My father was standing beside my bed and woke me up. I dressed myself quickly. Mother wanted to stop and save her jewel-case; but Father said: 'I refuse to let myself and my two children be burnt for the sake of your jewel-case.' We hurried downstairs, and as soon as I was outside I woke up."*

As the dream was a recurrent one, I naturally asked her when she had first dreamt it. She told me she did not know. But she remembered having had the dream three nights in succession at L—— (the place on the lake where the scene with Herr K. had taken place), and it had now come back again a few nights earlier, here in Vienna.[2] My expectations from the clearing-up of the dream were naturally heightened when I heard of its connection with the events at L——. But I wanted to discover first what had been the exciting cause of its recent recurrence, and I therefore asked Dora to take the dream bit by bit and tell me what occurred to her in connection with it. She had already had some training in dream interpretation from having previously analysed a few minor specimens.

"Something occurs to me," she said, "but it cannot belong to the dream, for it is quite recent, whereas I have certainly had the dream before."

---

[1] In answer to an inquiry Dora told me that there had never really been a fire at their house.

[2] The content of the dream makes it possible to establish that it in fact occurred *for the first time* at L——.

"That makes no difference," I replied. "Start away! It will simply turn out to be the most recent thing that fits in with the dream."

"Very well, then. Father has been having a dispute with Mother in the last few days, because she locks the dining-room door at night. My brother's room, you see, has no separate entrance, but can only be reached through the dining-room. Father does not want my brother to be locked in like that at night. He says it will not do: something might happen in the night so that it might be necessary to leave the room."

"And that made you think of the risk of fire?"

"Yes."

"Now, I should like you to pay close attention to the exact words you used. We may have to make use of them. You said that *'something might happen in the night so that it might be necessary to leave the room.'* "[3]

But Dora had now discovered the connecting link between the recent exciting cause of the dream and the original one, for she continued:

"When we arrived at L—— that time, Father and I, he openly said he was afraid of fire. We arrived in a violent thunderstorm, and saw the small wooden house without any lightning-conductor. So his anxiety was quite natural."

What I now had to do was to establish the relation between the events at L—— and the recurrent dreams which she had had there. I therefore said: "Did you have the dream during your first nights at L—— or during your last ones? In other words, before or after the scene in the wood by the lake of which we have heard so much?" (I must explain that I knew that the scene had not occurred on the very first day, and that she had remained at L—— for a few days after it without giving any hint of the incident.)

Her first reply was that she did not know, but after a while she added: "Yes. I think it was after the scene."

---

[3] I laid stress upon these words because they took me aback. They seemed to have an ambiguous ring about them. Are not certain physical exigencies referred to in the same words? Now, in a line of associations ambiguous words (or, as we may call them, "switch-words") act like points at a junction. If the points are switched across from the position in which they appear to lie in the dream, then we find ourselves upon another set of rails; and along this second track run the thoughts which we are in search of and which still lie concealed behind the dream.

So now I knew that the dream was a reaction to that experience. But why had it recurred there three times? I continued my questions: "How long did you stop on at L—— after the scene?"

"Four days more. On the fifth I went away with Father."

"Now I am certain that the dream was an immediate effect of your experience with Herr K. It was at L—— that you dreamed it for the first time, and not before. You have only introduced this uncertainty in your memory so as to obliterate the connection in your mind.[4] But the figures do not quite fit in to my satisfaction yet. If you stayed at L—— for four nights longer, the dream might have occurred four times over. Perhaps this was so?"

She no longer disputed my contention; but instead of answering my question she proceeded:[5] "In the afternoon after our trip on the lake, from which we (Herr K. and I) returned at midday, I had gone to lie down as usual on the sofa in the bedroom to have a short sleep. I suddenly awoke and saw Herr K. standing beside me. . . ."

"In fact, just as you saw your father standing beside your bed in the dream?"

"Yes. I asked him sharply what it was he wanted there. By way of reply he said he was not going to be prevented from coming into his own bedroom when he wanted; besides, there was something he wanted to fetch. This episode put me on my guard, and I asked Frau K. whether there was not a key to the bedroom door. The next morning (on the second day) I locked myself in while I was dressing. In the afternoon, when I wanted to lock myself in so as to lie down again on the sofa, the key was gone. I am convinced that Herr K. had removed it."

"Then here we have the theme of locking or not locking a room which appeared in the first association to the dream and also happened to occur in the exciting cause of the recent recurrence

---

[4]Compare what was said on p. 11 on the subject of doubt accompanying a recollection.

[5]This was because a fresh piece of material had to emerge from her memory before the question I had put could be answered.

of the dream.[6] I wonder whether the phrase '*I dressed myself quickly*' may not also belong to this context?"

"It was then that I made up my mind not to stay with Herr K. without Father. On the subsequent mornings I could not help feeling afraid that Herr K. would surprise me while I was dressing: *so I always dressed myself very quickly*. You see, Father lived at the hotel, and Frau K. used always to go out early so as to go on expeditions with him. But Herr K. did not annoy me again."

"I understand. On the afternoon of the second day after the scene in the wood you resolved to escape from his persecution, and during the second, third, and fourth nights you had time to repeat that resolution in your sleep. (You already knew on the second afternoon—before the dream, therefore—that you would not have the key on the following—the third—morning to lock yourself in with while you were dressing; and you could then form the design of dressing as quickly as possible.) But your dream recurred each night, for the very reason that it corresponded to a resolution. A resolution remains in existence until it has been carried out. You said to yourself, as it were: 'I shall have no rest and I can get no quiet sleep until I am out of this house.' In your account of the dream you turned it the other way and said: '*As soon as I was outside I woke up.*'"

At this point I shall interrupt my report of the analysis in order to compare this small piece of dream interpretation with the general statements I have made upon the mechanism of the formation of dreams. I argued in my book[7] that every dream is a wish which is represented as fulfilled, that the representation acts as a disguise if the wish is a repressed one, belonging to the unconscious, and

---

[6] I suspected, though I did not as yet say so to Dora, that she had seized upon this element on account of a symbolic meaning which it possessed. *"Zimmer"* ["room"] in dreams stands very frequently for *"Frauenzimmer"* [a slightly derogatory word for "woman"; literally, "women's apartments"]. The question whether a woman is "open" or "shut" can naturally not be a matter of indifference. It is well known, too, what sort of "key" effects the opening in such a case.

[7] *Die Traumdeutung*, 1900.

that except in the case of children's dreams only an unconscious wish or one which reaches down into the unconscious has the force necessary for the formation of a dream. I fancy my theory would have been more certain of general acceptance if I had contented myself with maintaining that every dream had a meaning, which could be discovered by means of a certain process of interpretation; and that when the interpretation had been completed the dream could be replaced by thoughts which would fall into place at an easily recognizable point in the waking mental life of the dreamer. I might then have gone on to say that the meaning of a dream turned out to be of as many different sorts as the processes of waking thought; that in one case it would be a fulfilled wish, in another a realized fear, or again a reflection persisting on into sleep, or a resolution (as in the instance of Dora's dream), or a piece of creative thought during sleep, and so on. Such a theory would no doubt have proved attractive from its very simplicity, and it might have been supported by a great many examples of dreams that had been satisfactorily interpreted, as for instance by the one which has been analysed in these pages.

But instead of this I formulated a generalization according to which the meaning of dreams is limited to a single form, to the representation of wishes, and by so doing I aroused a universal inclination to dissent. I must, however, observe that I did not consider it either my right or my duty to simplify a psychological process so as to make it more acceptable to my readers, when my researches had shown me that it presented a complication which could not be reduced to uniformity until the inquiry had been carried into another field. It is therefore of special importance to me to show that apparent exceptions—such as this dream of Dora's, which has shown itself in the first instance to be the continuation into sleep of a resolution formed during the day—nevertheless lend fresh support to the rule which is in dispute.

Much of the dream, however, still remained to be interpreted, and I proceeded with my questions: "What is this about the jewel-case that your mother wanted to save?"

"Mother is very fond of jewellery and had had a lot given her by Father."

"And you?"

"I used to be very fond of jewellery too, once; but I have not worn any since my illness.—Once, four years ago" (a year before the dream), "Father and Mother had a great dispute about a piece of jewellery. Mother wanted to be given a particular thing—pearl drops to wear in her ears. But Father does not like that kind of thing, and he brought her a bracelet instead of the drops. She was furious, and told him that as he had spent so much money on a present she did not like he had better just give it to some one else."

"I dare say you thought to yourself you would accept it with pleasure."

"I don't know.[8] I don't in the least know how Mother comes into the dream; she was not with us at L—— at the time."[9]

"I will explain that to you later. Does nothing else occur to you in connection with the jewel-case? So far you have only talked about jewellery and have said nothing about a case."

"Yes, Herr K. had made me a present of an expensive jewel-case a little time before."

"Then a return-present would have been very appropriate. Perhaps you do not know that 'jewel-case' ['*Schmuckkästchen*'] is a favourite expression for the same thing that you alluded to not long ago by means of the reticule you were wearing[10]—for the female genitals, I mean."

"I knew you would say that."[11]

"That is to say, you knew that it *was* so.—The meaning of the dream is now becoming even clearer. You said to yourself: 'This man is persecuting me; he wants to force his way into my room. My "jewel-case" is in danger, and if anything happens it will be Father's fault.' For that reason in the dream you chose a situation

---

[8] The regular formula with which she confessed to anything that had been repressed.

[9] This remark gave evidence of a complete misunderstanding of the rules of dream interpretation, though on other occasions Dora was perfectly familiar with them. This fact, coupled with the hesitancy and meagreness of her associations with the jewel-case, showed me that we were here dealing with material which had been very intensely repressed.

[10] This reference to the reticule will be explained further on.

[11] A very common way of putting aside a piece of knowledge that emerges from the repressed.

which expresses the opposite—a danger from which your father is saving you. In this part of the dream everything is turned into its opposite; you will soon discover why. As you say, the mystery turns upon your mother. You ask how she comes into the dream? She is, as you know, your former rival in your father's affections. In the incident of the bracelet, you would have been glad to accept what your mother had rejected. Now let us just put 'give' instead of 'accept' and 'withhold' instead of 'reject.' Then it means that you were ready to give your father what your mother withheld from him; and the thing in question was connected with jewellery.[12] Now bring your mind back to the jewel-case which Herr K. gave you. You have there the starting-point for a parallel line of thoughts, in which Herr K. is to be put in the place of your father just as he was in the matter of standing beside your bed. He gave you a jewel-case; so you are to give him your jewel-case. That was why I spoke just now of a 'return-present.' In this line of thoughts your mother must be replaced by Frau K. (You will not deny that she, at any rate, was present at the time.) So you are ready to give Herr K. what his wife withholds from him. That is the thought which has had to be repressed with so much energy, and which has made it necessary for every one of its elements to be turned into its opposite. The dream confirms once more what I had already told you before you dreamed it—that you are summoning up your old love for your father in order to protect yourself against your love for Herr K. But what do all these efforts show? Not only that you are afraid of Herr K., but that you are still more afraid of yourself, and of the temptation you feel to yield to him. In short, these efforts prove once more how deeply you loved him."[13]

Naturally Dora would not follow me in this part of the interpre-

---

[12]We shall be able later on to interpret even the drops in a way which will fit in with the context.

[13]I added: "Moreover, the re-appearance of the dream in the last few days forces me to the conclusion that you consider that the same situation has arisen once again, and that you have decided to give up the treatment—to which, after all, it is only your father who makes you come." The sequel showed how correct my guess had been. At this point my interpretation touches for a moment upon the subject of "transference"— a theme which is of the highest practical and theoretical importance, but into which I shall not have much further opportunity of entering in the present paper.

tation. I myself, however, had been able to arrive at a further step in the interpretation, which seemed to me indispensable both for the anamnesis of the case and for the theory of dreams. I promised to communicate this to Dora at the next sitting.

The fact was that I could not forget the hint which seemed to be conveyed by the ambiguous words already noticed—*that it might be necessary to leave the room; that an accident might happen in the night.* Added to this was the fact that the elucidation of the dream seemed to me incomplete so long as a particular requirement remained unsatisfied; for, though I do not wish to insist that this requirement is a universal one, I have a predilection for discovering a means of satisfying it. A regularly formed dream stands, as it were, upon two legs, one of which is in contact with the main and current exciting cause, and the other with some momentous occurrence in the years of childhood. The dream sets up a connection between those two factors—the event during childhood and the event of the present day—and it endeavours to re-shape the present upon the model of the remote past. For the wish which creates the dream always springs from the period of childhood; and it is continually trying to summon childhood back into reality and to correct the present day by the measure of childhood. I believed that I could already clearly detect the elements of Dora's dream, which could be pieced together into an allusion to an event in childhood.

I opened the discussion of the subject with a little experiment, which was, as usual, successful. There happened to be a large match-stand on the table. I asked Dora to look round and see whether she noticed anything special on the table, something that was not there as a rule. She noticed nothing. I then asked her if she knew why children were forbidden to play with matches.

"Yes; on account of the risk of fire. My uncle's children are very fond of playing with matches."

"Not only on that account. They are warned not to 'play with fire,' and a particular belief is associated with the warning."

She knew nothing about it.—"Very well, then; the fear is that if they do they will wet their bed. The antithesis of 'water' and 'fire' must be at the bottom of this. Perhaps it is believed that they will dream of fire and then try and put it out with water. I cannot say exactly. But I notice that the antithesis of water and fire has been extremely useful to you in the dream. Your mother wanted to save the jewel-case so that it should not be *burnt;* while in the dream-thoughts it is a question of the 'jewel-case' not being *wetted*. But fire is not only used as the contrary of water, it also serves directly to represent love (as in the phrase 'to be *consumed* with love'). So that from 'fire' one set of rails runs by way of this symbolic meaning to thoughts of love; while the other set runs by way of the contrary 'water,' and, after sending off a branch line which provides another connection with 'love' (for love also makes things wet), leads in a different direction. And what direction can that be? Think of the expressions you used: that *an accident might happen in the night,* and that *it might be necessary to leave the room*. Surely the allusion must be to a physical exigency? And if you transpose the accident into childhood what can it be but bed-wetting? But what is usually done to prevent children from wetting their bed? Are they not woken up in the night out of their sleep, *exactly as your father woke you up in the dream?* This, then, must be the actual occurrence which enabled you to substitute your father for Herr K., who really woke you up out of your sleep. I am accordingly driven to conclude that you were addicted to bed-wetting up to a later age than is usual with children. The same must also have been true of your brother; for your father said: *'I refuse to let my two children go to destruction. . . .'* Your brother has no other sort of connection with the real situation at the K.'s; he had not gone with you to L——. And now, what have your recollections to say to this?"

"I know nothing about myself," was her reply, "but my brother used to wet his bed up till his sixth or seventh year; and it used sometimes to happen to him in the daytime too."

I was on the point of remarking to her how much easier it is to remember things of that kind about one's brother than about oneself, when she continued the train of recollections which had been revived: "Yes. I used to do it too, for some time, but not until my seventh or eighth year. It must have been serious, because I remember now that the doctor was called in. It lasted till a short time before my nervous asthma."

"And what did the doctor say to it?"

"He explained it as nervous weakness; it would soon pass off, he thought; and he prescribed a tonic."[14]

The interpretation of the dream now seemed to me to be complete.[15] But Dora brought me an addendum to the dream on the very next day. She had forgotten to relate, she said, that each time after waking up she had smelt smoke. Smoke, of course, fitted in well with fire, but it also showed that the dream had a special relation to myself; for when she used to assert that there was nothing concealed behind this or that, I would often say by way of rejoinder: "There can be no smoke without fire!" Dora objected, however, to such a purely personal interpretation, saying that Herr K. and her father were passionate smokers—as I am too, for the matter of that. She herself had smoked during her stay by the lake, and Herr K. had rolled a cigarette for her before he began his unlucky proposal. She thought, too, that she clearly remembered noticing the smell of smoke on the three occasions of the dream's occurrence at L——, and not for the first time at its recent reappearance. As she would give me no further information, it was left to me to determine how this addendum was to be introduced into the texture of the dream-thoughts. One thing which I had to go upon was the fact that the smell of smoke had only come up as an addendum to the dream, and must therefore have had to overcome a particularly strong effort on the part of repression. Accordingly it was probably related to the thoughts which were the most obscurely presented and the most successfully repressed in the dream, to the thoughts, that is, concerned with the temptation to show herself willing to yield to the man. If that were so, the addendum to the dream could scarcely mean anything else than the longing for a kiss, which, with a smoker, would necessarily smell of smoke. But a kiss had passed between Herr K. and Dora some two years earlier, and it

---

[14]This physician was the only one in whom she showed any confidence, because this episode showed her that he had not penetrated her secret. She felt afraid of any other physician about whom she had not yet been able to form a judgement; and we can now see that the motive of her fear was the possibility that he might guess her secret.

[15]The essence of the dream might perhaps be translated into words such as these: "The temptation is so strong. Dear Father, protect me again as you used to in my childhood, and prevent my bed from being wetted!"

would certainly have been repeated more than once if she had given way to him. So the thoughts of temptation seemed in this way to have harked back to the earlier scene, and to have revived the memory of the kiss against whose seductive influence the little "suck-a-thumbs" had defended herself at the time by the feeling of disgust. Taking into consideration, finally, the indications which seemed to point to there having been a transference on to me—since I am a smoker too—I came to the conclusion that the idea had probably occurred to her one day during a sitting that she would like to have a kiss from me. This would have been the exciting cause which led her to repeat the warning dream and to form her resolution of stopping the treatment. Everything fits together very satisfactorily upon this view; but owing to the characteristics of "transference" its validity is not susceptible of definite proof.

I might at this point hesitate whether I should first consider the light thrown by this dream upon the history of the case, or whether I should rather begin by dealing with the objection to my theory of dreams which may be based upon it. I shall take the former course.

The significance of bed-wetting in the early history of neurotics is worth going into thoroughly. For the sake of clearness I will confine myself to remarking that Dora's case of bed-wetting was not the usual one. The disorder was not simply that the habit had persisted beyond what is considered the normal period, but, according to her explicit account, it had begun by disappearing and had then returned at a relatively late age—after her sixth year. Bedwetting of this kind has, to the best of my knowledge, no more likely cause than masturbation, a habit whose importance in the aetiology of bed-wetting in general is still insufficiently appreciated. In my experience, the children concerned have themselves at one time been very well aware of this connection, and all its psychological consequences follow from it as though they had never forgotten it. Now, at the time when Dora reported the dream, we were engaged upon a line of inquiry which led straight towards an admission that she had masturbated in childhood. A short while before, she had raised the question of why it was precisely *she* that had fallen ill, and, before I could answer, had put the blame on her father. The justification for this was forthcoming not out of her unconscious thoughts but from her conscious knowledge. It turned out, to my astonishment, that the girl knew what the nature of her father's illness had been. After his return from consulting me she had overheard a conversation in which the name of the disease had been mentioned. At a still earlier period—at the time of the detached retina—an oculist who was called in must have hinted at a luetic aetiology; for the inquisitive and anxious girl overheard an old aunt of hers saying to her mother: "He was ill before his marriage, you know," and adding something which she could not understand, but which she subsequently connected in her mind with improper subjects.

Her father, then, had fallen ill through leading a loose life, and she assumed that he had handed on his bad health to her by heredity. I was careful not to tell her that, as I have already mentioned (see pp. 15f), I was of opinion, too, that the offspring of luetics were very specially predisposed to severe neuro-psychoses. The line of thought in which she brought this accusation against her father was continued in her unconscious material. For several days on end she identified herself with her mother by means of slight symptoms and peculiarities of manner, which gave her an opportunity for some really remarkable achievements in the direction of intolerable behaviour. She then allowed it to transpire that she was thinking of a stay she had made at Franzensbad, which she had visited with her mother—I forget in what year. Her mother was suffering from abdominal pains and from a discharge (a catarrh) which necessitated a cure at Franzensbad. It was Dora's view—and here again she was probably right—that this illness was due to her father, who had thus handed on his venereal disease to her mother. It was quite natural that in drawing this conclusion she should, like the majority of laymen, have confused gonorrhoea and syphilis—what is contagious and what is hereditary. The persistence with which she held to this identification with her mother forced me almost to ask her whether she too was suffering from a venereal disease; and I then learnt that she was afflicted with a catarrh (leucorrhoea) whose beginning, she said, she could not remember.

I then understood that behind the train of thought in which she brought these open accusations against her father there lay concealed as usual a self-accusation. I met her half-way by assuring her that in my view the occurrence of leucorrhoea in young girls pointed primarily to masturbation, and I considered that all the other causes which were commonly assigned to that complaint were put in the background by masturbation.[16] I added that she was now on the way to finding an answer to her own question of why it was precisely *she* that had fallen ill—by confessing that she had masturbated, probably in childhood. Dora denied flatly that she could remember any such thing. But a few days later she did something which I could not help regarding as a further step towards the confession. For on that day she wore at her waist—a thing she never did on any other occasion before or after—a small reticule of a shape which had just come into fashion; and, as she lay on the sofa and talked, she kept playing with it—opening it, putting a finger into it, shutting it again, and so on. I looked on for some time, and then explained to her the nature of a *symptomatic act*.[17] I give the name of symptomatic acts to those acts which people perform, as we say, automatically, unconsciously, without attending to them, or as if in a moment of distraction. They are actions to which people would like to deny any significance, and which, if questioned about them, they would explain as being indifferent and accidental. Closer observation, however, will show that these actions, about which consciousness knows nothing or wishes to know nothing, in fact give expression to unconscious thoughts and impulses, and are therefore most valuable and instructive as being manifestations of the unconscious which have been able to come to the surface. There are two sorts of conscious attitudes possible towards these symptomatic acts. If we can ascribe inconspicuous motives to them we recognize their existence; but if no such pretext can be found for conscious use we usually fail altogether to notice that we have performed them. Dora found no difficulty in producing a motive: "Why should I not wear a reticule like this, as it is now the fashion to do?" But a justification of this kind does not dismiss the possibility of the action in ques-

---

[16](*Additional Note*, 1923).—This is an extreme view which I should no longer maintain today.

[17]See my paper upon the psycho-pathology of everyday life in the *Monatsschrift für Psychiatrie und Neurologie*, 1901 (published in book form in 1904).

tion having an unconscious origin. Though on the other hand the existence of such an origin and the meaning attributed to the act cannot be conclusively established. We must content ourselves with recording the fact that such a meaning fits in quite extraordinarily well with the situation as a whole and with the order of the day as laid down by the unconscious.

On some other occasion I will publish a collection of these symptomatic acts as they are to be observed in the healthy and in neurotics. They are sometimes very easy to interpret. Dora's reticule, which came apart at the top in the usual way, was nothing but a representation of the genitals, and her playing with it, her opening it and putting her finger in it, was an entirely unembarrassed yet unmistakable pantomimic announcement of what she would like to do with them—namely, to masturbate. A very entertaining episode of a similar kind occurred to me a short time ago. In the middle of a sitting the patient—a lady who was no longer young—brought out a small ivory box, ostensibly in order to refresh herself with a sweet. She made some efforts to open it, and then handed it to me so that I might convince myself how hard it was to open. I expressed my suspicion that the box must mean something special, for this was the very first time I had seen it, although its owner had been coming to me for more than a year. To this the lady eagerly replied: "I always have this box about me; I take it with me wherever I go." She did not calm down until I had pointed out to her with a laugh how well her words were adapted to quite another meaning. The box—*Dose, Pyxis*—like the reticule and the jewel-case, was once again only a substitute for the shell of Venus, for the female genitals.

There is a great deal of symbolism of this kind in life, but as a rule we pass it by without heeding it. When I set myself the task of bringing to light what human beings keep hidden within them, not by the compelling power of hypnosis, but by observing what they say and what they show, I thought the task was a harder one than it really is. He that has eyes to see and ears to hear may convince himself that no mortal can keep a secret. If his lips are silent, he chatters with his finger-tips; betrayal oozes out of him at every pore. And thus the task of making conscious the most hidden recesses of the mind is one which it is quite possible to accomplish.

Dora's symptomatic act with the reticule did not immediately precede the dream. She started the sitting which brought us the narrative of the dream with another symptomatic act. As I came into the room in which she was waiting she hurriedly concealed a letter which she was reading. I naturally asked her whom the letter was from, and at first she refused to tell me. Something then came out which was a matter of complete indifference and had no relation to the treatment. It was a letter from her grandmother, in which she begged Dora to write to her more often. I believe that Dora only wanted to play "secrets" with me, and to hint that she was on the point of allowing her secret to be torn from her by the physician. I was then in a position to explain her antipathy to every new physician. She was afraid lest he might arrive at the foundation of her illness, either by examining her and discovering her catarrh, or by questioning her and eliciting the fact of her addiction to bed-wetting—lest he might guess, in short, that she had masturbated. And afterwards she would speak very contemptuously of the physicians whose perspicacity she had evidently over-estimated beforehand.

The reproaches against her father for having made her ill, together with the self-reproach underlying them, the leucorrhoea, the playing with the reticule, the bed-wetting after her sixth year, the secret which she would not allow the physicians to tear from her—the circumstantial evidence of her having masturbated in childhood seems to me complete and without a flaw. In the present case I had begun to suspect the masturbation when she had told me of her cousin's gastric pains (see p. 31), and had then identified herself with her by complaining for days together of similar painful sensations. It is well known that gastric pains occur especially often in those who masturbate. According to a personal communication made to me by W. Fliess, it is precisely gastralgias of this character which can be interpreted by an application of cocaine to the "gastric spot" discovered by him in the nose, and which can be cured by the cauterization of the same spot. In confirmation of my suspicion Dora gave me two facts from her conscious knowledge: she herself had frequently suffered from gastric pains, and she had good reasons for believing that her cousin was a masturbator. It is a very common thing for patients to recognize in other people a connection which, on account of their emotional resistances, they cannot perceive in themselves. And, indeed, Dora no longer denied my supposition, although she still remembered nothing. Even the date which she assigned to the bed-wetting, when she said that it lasted "till a short time before the appearance of the nervous asthma," appears to me to be of clinical significance. Hysterial symptoms hardly ever appear so long as children are masturbating, but only afterwards, when a period of abstinence has set in;[18] they form a substitute for masturbatory satisfaction, the desire for which continues to persist in the unconscious until another and more normal kind of satisfaction appears—where that is still attainable. For upon whether it is still attainable or not depends the possibility of a hysteria being cured by marriage and normal sexual intercourse. But if the satisfaction afforded in marriage is again removed—as it may be owing to *coitus interruptus,* psychological estrangement, or other causes—then the libido flows back again into its old channel and manifests itself once more in hysterical symptoms.

I should like to be able to add some definite information as to when and under what particular influence Dora gave up masturbating; but owing to the incompleteness of the analysis I have only fragmentary material to present. We have heard that the bed-wetting lasted until shortly before she first fell ill with dyspnoea. Now the only light she was able to throw upon this first attack was that at the time of its occurrence her father was away from home for the first time since his health had improved. In this small recollection there must be a trace of an allusion to the aetiology of the dyspnoea. Dora's symptomatic acts and certain other signs gave me good reasons for supposing that the child, whose bedroom had been next door to her parents', had overheard her father in his wife's room at night and had heard him (for he was always short of breath) breathing hard during their coitus. Children, in such circumstances, divine something sexual in the uncanny sounds that reach their ears. Indeed, the movements expressive of sexual excitement lie within them ready to hand, as innate pieces of mecha-

---

[18]This is also true in principle of adults; but in their case a relative abstinence, a diminution in the amount of masturbation, is a sufficient cause, so that, if the libido is very strong, hysteria and masturbation may be simultaneously present.

nism. I maintained years ago that the dyspnoea and palpitations that occur in hysteria and anxiety-neurosis are only detached fragments of the act of copulation; and in many cases, as in Dora's, I have been able to trace back the symptom of dyspnoea or nervous asthma to the same exciting cause—to the patient's having overheard sexual intercourse taking place between adults. The sympathetic excitement which may be supposed to have occurred in Dora on such an occasion may very easily have made the child's sexuality veer round and have replaced her inclination to masturbation by an inclination to morbid anxiety. A little while later, when her father was away and the child, devotedly in love with him, was wishing him back, she must have reproduced in the form of an attack of asthma the impression she had received. She had preserved in her memory the event which had occasioned the first onset of the symptom, and we can conjecture from it the nature of the train of thought, charged with anxiety, which had accompanied the attack. The first attack had come on after she had over-exerted herself on an expedition in the mountains, so that she had probably been really a little out of breath. To this was added the thought that her father was forbidden to climb mountains and was not allowed to over-exert himself, because he suffered from shortness of breath; then came the recollection of how much he had exerted himself with her mother that night, and the question whether it might not have done him harm; next came concern whether she might not have overexerted herself in masturbating—an act which, like the other, led to a sexual orgasm accompanied by slight dyspnoea—and finally came a return of the dyspnoea in an intensified form as a symptom. Part of this material I was able to obtain directly from the analysis, but the rest required supplementing. And, indeed, the method by which the occurrence of masturbation in Dora's case has been verified has shown us that material belonging to a single subject can only be collected piece by piece at various times and in different connections.[19]

---

[19]The proof of infantile masturbation in other cases is established in a precisely similar way. The evidence for it is mostly of a similar nature: indications of the presence of leucorrhoea, bed-wetting, hand-ceremonials (obsessional washing), and such things. It is always possible to discover with certainty from the nature of the symptoms of the case whether the habit was discovered by the person in charge of the child or not, or

There now arise a whole series of questions of the greatest importance concerning the aetiology of hysteria: is Dora's case to be regarded as aetiologically typical? does it represent the only type of causation? and so on. Nevertheless, I am sure that I am taking the right course in postponing my answer to such questions until a considerable number of other cases have been similarly analysed and published. Moreover, I should have to begin by criticizing the way in which the questions are framed. Instead of answering "Yes" or "No" to the question whether the aetiology of this case is to be looked for in masturbation during childhood, I should first have to discuss the concept of aetiology as applied to the psychoneuroses. It would then become evident that the standpoint from which I should be able to answer the question would be very widely removed from the standpoint from which it was put. Let it suffice if we can reach the conviction that in this case the occurrence of masturbation in childhood is established, and that its occurrence cannot be an accidental element nor an immaterial one in the conformation of the clinical picture.[20]

---

whether this sexual activity was brought to an end by long efforts on the child's part to break itself of the habit, or by a sudden change. In Dora's case the masturbation had remained undiscovered, and had come to an end at a single blow (cf. her secret, her fear of doctors, and the replacement by dyspnoea). The patients, it is true, invariably dispute the conclusiveness of circumstantial evidence such as this, and they do so even when they have retained a conscious recollection of the catarrh or of their mother's warning (e.g. "That makes people stupid; it's dangerous"). But some time later the memory, which has been so long repressed, of this piece of infantile sexual life emerges with certainty, and it does so in every instance. I am reminded of the case of a patient of mine suffering from obsessions, which are direct derivatives of infantile masturbation. Her peculiarities, such as self-prohibitions and self-punishments, the feeling that if she has done this she must not do that, the idea that she must not be interrupted, the introduction of pauses between one procedure (with her hands) and the next, her hand-washing, etc.—all of these turned out to be unaltered fragments of her nurse's efforts to break her of the habit. The only thing which had remained permanently in her memory were the words of warning: "Ugh! That's dangerous!" Compare also in this connection my *Drei Abhandlungen zur Sexualtheorie*, 1905.

[20]Dora's brother must have been concerned in some way with her having acquired the habit of masturbation; for in this connection she told me, with all the emphasis which betrays the presence of a "screen-memory," that her brother used regularly to pass on all his infectious illnesses to her, and that while he used to have them lightly she used, on the contrary, to have them severely. In the dream her brother as well as she was saved from "destruction"; he, too, had been subject to bed-wetting, but had got over the habit before his sister. Her declaration that she had been able to keep abreast with her brother up to the time of her first illness, but that after that she had fallen behind him in her studies, was in a certain sense also a "screen-memory." It

A consideration of the significance of the leucorrhoea to which Dora admitted promises to give us a still better understanding of her symptoms. She had learnt to call her affection a "catarrh" at the time when her mother had had to visit Franzensbad on account of a similar complaint; and the word "catarrh" acted once again as a "switchword," and enabled the whole set of thoughts upon her father's responsibility for her illness to manifest themselves in the symptom of the cough. The cough, which no doubt originated in the first instance from a slight actual catarrh, was, moreover, an imitation of her father (whose lungs were affected), and could serve as an expression of her sympathy and concern for him. But besides this, it proclaimed aloud, as it were, something of which she may then have been still unconscious: "I am my father's daughter. I have a catarrh, just as he has. He has made me ill, just as he has made Mother ill. It is from him that I have got my evil passions, which are punished by illness."[21]

We will now attempt to put together the various determinants that we have found for Dora's attacks of coughing and hoarseness. In the lowest stratum we must assume the presence of a real and organically determined irritation of the throat—which acted like the grain of sand around which an oyster forms its pearl. This irritation was susceptible to fixation, because it concerned a part of the body which in Dora had to a high degree retained its significance as an erotogenic zone. And the irritation was consequently well fitted to give expression to excited states of the libido.

---

was as though she had been a boy up till that moment, and had then become girlish for the first time. She had in truth been a wild creature; but after the "asthma" she became quiet and well-behaved. That illness formed the boundary between two phases of her sexual life, of which the first was masculine in character, and the second feminine.

[21] This word ("catarrh") played the same part with the twelve-year-old girl whose case history I have compressed into a few lines. I had established the child in a pension with an intelligent lady, who took charge of her for me. The lady reported that the little girl could not bear her to be in the room while she was going to bed, and that when she was in bed she had a marked cough, of which there was no trace in the daytime. When the girl was questioned about these symptoms, the only thing that occurred to her was that her grandmother coughed in the same way, and that she was said to have a catarrh. It was clear from this that the child herself had a catarrh, and that she did not want to be observed while she performed her evening ablutions. This catarrh, which, thanks to its name, had been *displaced from below upwards*, even exhibited an unusual degree of intensity.

It was brought to fixation by what was probably its first psychological wrapping—her sympathetic imitation of her father—and by her subsequent self-reproaches on account of her "catarrh." The same group of symptoms, moreover, showed itself capable of representing her relations with Herr K.; it could express her regret at his absence and her wish to make him a better wife. After a part of her libido had once more turned towards her father, the symptom obtained what was perhaps its last meaning; it came to represent sexual intercourse with her father by means of Dora's identifying herself with Frau K. I can guarantee that this series is by no means complete. Unfortunately, an incomplete analysis cannot enable us to follow the temporal sequence of the changes in a symptom's meaning, or to display clearly the succession and coexistence of its various meanings. It may legitimately be expected of a complete analysis that it should fulfil these demands.

I must now proceed to touch upon some further relations existing between Dora's genital catarrh and her hysterical symptoms. At a time when any psychological elucidation of hysteria was still very remote, I used to hear experienced fellow-doctors who were my seniors maintain that in the case of hysterical patients suffering from leucorrhoea any increase in the catarrh was regularly followed by an intensification of the hysterical troubles, and especially of anorexia and vomiting. No one was very clear about the nature of the connection, but I fancy the general inclination was towards the opinion held by gynaecologists. According to their hypothesis, as is well known, disorders of the genitals exercise upon the nervous functions a direct and far-reaching influence in the nature of an organic disturbance—though a therapeutic test of this theory is apt to leave one in the lurch. In the light of our present knowledge we cannot exclude the possibility of the existence of a direct organic influence of this sort; but it is at all events easier to determine its psychological wrappings. The pride taken by women in the appearance of their genitals is quite a special feature of their vanity; and disorders of the genitals which they think calculated to inspire feelings of repugnance or even disgust have an incredible power of humiliating them, of lowering their self-esteem, and of making them irritable, sensitive, and distrustful. An abnormal secretion of the mucous membrane of the vagina is looked upon as a source of disgust.

It will be remembered that Dora had a lively feeling of disgust after being kissed by Herr K., and that we saw grounds for completing her story of the scene of the kiss by supposing that, while she was being embraced, she noticed the pressure of the man's erect member against her body. We now learn further that the same governess whom Dora cast off on account of her faithlessness had, from her own experience of life, propounded to Dora the view that all men were frivolous and untrustworthy. To Dora that must mean that all men were like her father. But she thought her father suffered from venereal disease—for had he not handed it on to her and her mother? She might therefore have imagined to herself that all men suffered from venereal disease, and naturally her conception of venereal disease was modelled upon her one experience of it—a personal one at that. To suffer from venereal disease, therefore, meant for her to be afflicted with a disgusting discharge. So may we not have here a further motive for the disgust she felt at the moment of the embrace? Thus the disgust which was transferred on to the contact of the man would be a feeling which had been projected according to the primitive mechanism I have already mentioned (see p. 28), and would be related ultimately to her own leucorrhoea.

I suspect that we are here concerned with unconscious processes of thought which are twined around a pre-existing structure of organic connections, much as festoons of flowers are twined around a wire; so that on another occasion one might find other lines of thought inserted between the same points of departure and termination. Yet a knowledge of the thought-connections which have been effective in the individual case is of a value which cannot be exaggerated for clearing up the symptoms. It is only because the analysis was prematurely broken off that we have been obliged in Dora's case to resort to framing conjectures and filling in deficiencies. What I have brought forward for filling up the gaps is invariably supported by other cases which have been more thoroughly analysed.

The dream from the analysis of which we have derived this information corresponded, as we have seen, to a resolution which Dora carried with her into her sleep. It was therefore repeated each night until the resolution had been carried out; and it reappeared years later when an occasion arose for forming an analogous resolution. The resolution might have been consciously expressed in some such words as these: "I must fly from this house, for I see that my virginity is threatened here; I shall go away with my father, and I shall take precautions not to be surprised while I am dressing in the morning." These thoughts are clearly expressed in the dream; they form part of a mental current which has achieved consciousness and a dominating position in waking life. Behind them can be discerned obscure traces of a train of thought which forms part of a contrary current and has consequently been suppressed. This other train of thought culminated in the temptation to yield to the man, out of gratitude for the love and tenderness he had shown her during the last few years, and it may perhaps have revived the memory of the only kiss she had so far had from him. But according to the theory which I developed in my *Traumdeutung* such elements as these are not enough for the formation of a dream. On that theory a dream is not a resolution represented as having been carried out, but a wish represented as having been fulfilled, and, moreover, in most cases a wish dating from childhood. It is our business now to discover whether this principle may not be contradicted by the present dream.

The dream does in fact contain infantile material, though it is impossible at a first glance to discover any connection between that material and Dora's resolution to fly from Herr K.'s house and the temptation of his presence. Why should a recollection have emerged of her bed-wetting when she was a child and of the trouble her father used to take to teach the child clean habits? We may answer this by saying that it was only by the help of this train of thought that it was possible to suppress the other thoughts which were so intensely occupied with the temptation to yield, or that it was possible to secure the domination of the resolution which had been formed to combat those other thoughts. The child decided to fly *with* her father; in reality she fled *to* her father because she was afraid of the man who was pursuing her; she summoned up an infantile affection for her father so that it might protect her against her present affection for a stranger. Her father was himself partly responsible for her present danger, for he had handed her over to this strange man in the interests of his own love-affair. And how much better it had been when that same father of hers had loved no one more than her, and had exerted all his strength to save her from the dangers that had then threatened her. The infantile, and now unconscious, wish to put her father in the strange man's place had the potency necessary for the formation of a dream. If there had been a past situation similar to a present one, and differing from it only in being concerned with one instead of with the other of the two persons mentioned in the wish, that situation would become the main one in the dream. But there *had* been such a situation. Her father had once stood beside her bed, just as Herr K. had the day before, and had woken her up, with a kiss perhaps, as Herr K. may have intended to do. Thus her resolution to fly from the house was not in itself capable of producing a dream; but it became so by being associated with another resolution which was founded upon infantile wishes. The wish to replace Herr K. by her father provided the necessary motive power for the dream. Let me recall the interpretation I was led to adopt of Dora's intensified train of thought about her father's relations with Frau K. My interpretation was that she had at that point summoned up an infantile affection for her father so as to be able to keep her repressed love for Herr K. in its state of repression. This same sudden revulsion in the patient's mental life was reflected in the dream.

I have made one or two observations in my *Traumdeutung*[22] upon the relation between the waking thoughts (day's residues) which are continued into sleep and the unconscious wish which forms the dream. I will quote them here as they stand, for I have nothing to add to them, and the analysis of this dream of Dora's proves afresh that the facts are as I have supposed.

"I admit that there is a whole class of dreams the *instigation* to which comes mainly or even exclusively from the residues of waking life; and I think that even my wish to become—at length

---

[22]Seventh Edition, p.416.

and at last—a Professor Extraordinarius[23] might have allowed me a quiet night's sleep, if the concern I had felt during the day about my friend's health had not continued to be active. But the concern by itself would not have produced a dream; the *motive power* required for a dream had to be contributed by a wish; and it lay with the concern to provide itself with a wish which would act as the motive power for the dream. To use a simile: it is quite possible for a thought from waking life to play the part of an *entrepreneur* for a dream. But the *entrepreneur,* who, as they say, has an idea and thirsts to put it into effect, can nevertheless do nothing without capital. He needs a capitalist to meet the expenses; and this capitalist, who can supply the psychological outlay for the dream, is invariably and inevitably, whatever the thought from waking life may be, *a wish from the unconscious.*"

Any one who has learnt to appreciate the delicacy of the fabric of structures such as dreams will not be surprised to find that Dora's wish that her father might take the place of the man who was her tempter called up in her memory not merely a casual collection of material from her childhood, but precisely such material as was most intimately bound up with the suppression of her temptation. For if Dora felt unable to yield to her love for the man, if in the end she repressed that love instead of surrendering to it, there was no factor upon which her decision depended more directly than upon her premature sexual enjoyment and its consequences—her bed-wetting, her catarrh, and her disgust. An early history of this kind can afford a basis for two kinds of behaviour in response to the demands of love in maturity—which of the two will depend upon the summation of constitutional determinants in the individual. He will either exhibit an abandonment to sexuality which is entirely without resistances and borders upon perversity; or there will be a reaction—he will repudiate sexuality, and will at the same time fall ill of a neurosis. In the case of our present patient, her constitution and the high level of her intellectual and moral education decided in favour of the latter course.

I should like, further, to draw special attention to the fact that

---

[23]This refers to the analysis of a dream quoted in the book as an example.

the analysis of this dream has given us access to certain details of the pathogenically operative events which had otherwise been inaccessible to memory, or at all events to reproduction. The recollection of the bed-wetting in childhood had, as we have seen, already been repressed. And Dora had never mentioned the details of her perscution by Herr K.; they had never occurred to her mind.

I add a few remarks which may help towards the synthesis of this dream. The dream-work began on the afternoon of the second day after the scene in the wood, after Dora had noticed that she was no longer able to lock the door of her room. She then said to herself: "I am threatened by a serious danger here," and formed her resolution not to stop on in the house alone but to go off with her father. This resolution became capable of forming a dream, because it succeeded in finding a continuation in the unconscious. What corresponded to it there was her summoning up her infantile love for her father as a protection against the present temptation. The change which thus took place in her became fixed and brought her into the attitude shown by her supervalent train of thought— jealousy of Frau K. on her father's account, as though she herself were in love with him. There was a conflict within her between a temptation to yield to the man's proposal and a composite force rebelling against that feeling. This latter force was made up of motives of respectability and good sense, of hostile feelings caused by the governess's disclosures (jealousy and wounded pride, as we shall see later), and of a neurotic element, namely, the tendency to a repudiation of sexuality which was already present in her and was based upon the story of her childhood. Her love for her father, which she summoned up to protect her against the temptation, had its origin in this same story of her childhood.

Her resolution of flying to her father, which, as we have seen, reached down into the unconscious, was transformed by the dream into a situation which presented as fulfilled the wish that her father should save her from the danger. In this process it was necessary to put on one side a certain thought which stood in the way; for it was her father himself who had brought her into the danger.

The hostile feeling against her father (her desire for revenge), which was here suppressed, was, as we shall discover, one of the motive forces of the second dream.

According to the conditions of dream formation the imagined situation must be chosen so as to reproduce a situation in infancy. A special triumph is achieved if a recent situation, perhaps even the very situation which is the exciting cause of the dream, can be transformed into an infantile one. This has actually been achieved in the present case, by a purely chance disposition of the material. Just as Herr K. had stood beside her sofa and woken her up, so her father had often done in her childhood. The whole trend of her thoughts could be most aptly symbolized by her substitution of her father for Herr K. in that situation.

But the reason for which her father used to wake her up long ago had been to prevent her from making her bed wet.

This "wet" had a decisive influence upon the further content of the dream; though it was represented in it only by a distant allusion and by its opposite.

The opposite of "wet" and "water" can easily be "fire" and "burning." The chance that, when they arrived at the place, her father had expressed his anxiety at the risk of fire, helped to decide that the danger from which her father was to rescue her should be a fire. The situation chosen for the dream-picture was based upon this chance, and upon the opposition to "wet": "There was a fire. Her father was standing beside her bed to wake her." Her father's chance utterance would, no doubt, not have obtained such an important position in the dream if it had not fitted in so excellently with the dominating current of feeling, which was determined to regard him at any cost as a protector and saviour. "He foresaw the danger from the very moment of our arrival! He was in the right!" (As a matter of fact, it was he who had brought the girl into danger.)

In consequence of certain connections which can easily be made from it, the word "wet" served in the dream-thoughts as a point of junction between several groups of ideas. "Wet" was connected not only with the bed-wetting, but also with the group of ideas relating to sexual temptation which lay suppressed behind the content of the dream. Dora knew that there was a kind of getting wet involved in sexual intercourse, and that during the act of copulation the man presented the woman with something liquid *in the form of drops*. She also knew that the danger lay precisely in that, and that it was her business to protect her genitals from being moistened.

"Wet" and "drops" at the same time opened the way to the other group of associations—the group relating to the disgusting catarrh, which in her later years had no doubt possessed the same mortifying significance for her as the bed-wetting had in her childhood. "Wet" in this connection had the same meaning as "dirtied." Her genitals, which ought to have been kept clean, had really been dirtied already by the catarrh—and this applied to her mother no less than to herself (see p. 67). She seemed to understand that her mother's mania for cleanliness was a reaction against this dirtying.

The two groups of ideas met in this one thought: "Mother got both things from father: the sexual wetness and the dirtying discharge." Dora's jealousy of her mother was inseparable from the group of thoughts relating to her infantile love for her father which she summoned up for her protection. But this material was not yet capable of representation. If, however, a recollection could be found which was equally closely connected with both the groups related to the word "wet," but which avoided any offensiveness, then such a recollection would be able to take over the representation in the dream of the material in question.

A recollection of this sort was furnished by the episode of the "drops"—the jewellery [*"Schmuck"*] that Dora's mother wanted to have. In appearance the connection between this reminiscence and the two groups of thoughts relating to sexual wetness and to being dirtied was a purely external and superficial one, of a verbal character. For "drops" was used ambiguously as a "switchword," while "jewellery" [*"Schmuck"*] was taken as an equivalent to "clean," and thus as a rather forced contrary of "dirtied."[24] But in reality the most substantial connections can be

---

[24][The German word *"Schmuck"* has a much wider meaning than the English "jewellery," though that is the sense in which it occurs in the compound *"Schmuckkästchen,"* "jewel-case." As a substantive, *"Schmuck"* denotes "finery" of all kinds, not only personal adornments, but embellishments of objects and decorations in general. As an adjective, it can mean "smart," "tidy," or "neat."—*Trans.*]

shown to have existed between the things denoted themselves. The recollection originated from the material connected with Dora's jealousy of her mother, which, though its roots were infantile, had persisted far beyond that period. By means of these two word-bridges it was possible to transfer on to the single reminiscence of the "jewel-drops" the whole of the significance attaching to the ideas of her parents' sexual intercourse, and of her mother's gonorrhoea and tormenting passion for cleanliness.

But a still further displacement had to be effected before this material appeared in the dream. Though "drops" is nearer to the original "wet," it was the more distant "jewellery" that found a place in the dream. When, therefore, this element had been inserted into the dream situation which had already been determined the account might have run: "Mother wanted to stop and save her jewellery." But a subsequent influence now made itself felt, and led to the further alteration of "jewellery" into "jewel-case." This influence came from elements in the underlying group relating to the temptation offered by Herr K. Herr K. had never given her jewellery, but he had given her a "case" for it, which represented for Dora all the marks of preference and all the tenderness for which she felt she ought now to have been grateful. And the composite word thus formed, "jewel-case," had beyond this a special claim to be used as a representative element in the dream. Is not "jewel-case" ["*Schmuckkästchen*"] a term commonly used to describe female genitals that are immaculate and intact? And is it not, on the other hand, an innocent word? Is it not, in short, admirably calculated both to betray and to conceal the sexual thoughts that lie behind the dream?

"Mother's jewel-case" was therefore introduced in two places in the dream; and this element replaced all mention of Dora's infantile jealousy, of the drops (that is, of the sexual wetness), of being dirtied by the discharge, and, on the other hand, of her present thoughts connected with the temptation—the thoughts which were urging her to reciprocate the man's love, and which depicted the sexual situation (alike desirable and menacing) that lay before her. The element of "jewel-case" was more than any other a product of condensation and displacement, and a compro-

mise between contrary mental currents. The multiplicity of its origin—both from infantile and contemporary sources—is no doubt
pointed to by its double appearance in the content of the dream.

The dream was a reaction to a fresh experience of an exciting
nature; and this experience must inevitably have revived the memory
of the only previous experience which was at all analogous to it. The
latter was the scene of the kiss in Herr K.'s place of business, when
she had been seized with disgust. But this same scene was associatively accessible from other directions too, namely, from the group
of thoughts relating to the catarrh (see p. 75), and from her present
temptation. The scene therefore brought to the dream a contribution
of its own, which had to be made to fit in with the dream situation
that had already been determined: "There was a fire" . . . no doubt
the kiss smelt of smoke; so she smelt smoke in the dream, and the
smell persisted till after she was awake.

By inadvertence, I unfortunately left a gap in the analysis of the
dream. Dora's father was made to say, "I refuse to let my two
children go to destruction . . ." ("as a result of masturbation"
should no doubt be added from the dream-thoughts). Such speeches
in dreams are regularly constructed out of pieces of actual speeches
which have either been made or heard. I ought to have made inquiries
as to the actual source of this speech. The results of my inquiry would
have shown that the structure of the dream was more complicated, but
would at the same time have made it easier to penetrate.

Are we to suppose that when this dream occurred at L—— it had
precisely the same content as when it recurred during the treatment?
It does not seem necessary to do so. Experience shows that people
often assert that they have had the same dream, when as a matter of
fact the separate appearances of the recurrent dream have differed
from one another in numerous details and in other respects that were
of no small importance. Thus one of my patients told me that she
had had her favourite dream again the night before, and that it always
recurred in the same form: she had dreamed of swimming in the blue
sea, of joyfully parting the waves, and so on. On closer investigation
it turned out that upon a common background now one detail and
now another was brought out; on one occasion, even, she was swimming in a frozen sea and was surrounded by icebergs. This patient

had other dreams, which turned out to be closely connected with the recurrent one, though even she made no attempt to claim that they were identical with it. Once, for instance, she was looking at a view (based on a photograph, but life-size) which showed the Upper Town and the Lower Town in Heligoland simultaneously; on the sea was a ship, in which were two people whom she had known in her youth, and so on.

What is certain is that in Dora's case the dream which occurred during the treatment had gained a new significance connected with the present time, though perhaps its manifest content had not changed. The dream-thoughts behind it included a reference to my treatment, and it corresponded to a renewal of the old resolution to withdraw from a danger. If her memory was not deceiving her when she declared that even at L—— she had noticed the smoke after she woke up, it must be acknowledged that she had brought my proverb, "There can be no smoke without fire," very ingeniously into the completed form of the dream, in which it seemed to serve as an over-determination of the last element. It was undeniably a mere matter of chance that the most recent exciting cause—her mother's locking the dining-room door so that her brother was shut into his bedroom—had provided a connection with her persecution by Herr K. at L——, where her resolution had been formed when she found she could not lock her bedroom door. It is possible that her brother did not appear in the dream on the earlier occasions, so that the words "my two children" did not form part of its content until after the occurrence of its latest exciting cause.

4. The Second Dream

A few weeks after the first dream the second occurred, and when it had been dealt with the analysis was broken off. It cannot be made as completely intelligible as the first, but it afforded a desirable confirmation of an assumption which had become necessary about the patient's mental state, it filled up a gap in her memory, and it made it possible to obtain a deep insight into the origin of another of her symptoms.

Dora described the dream as follows: *"I was walking about in a town which I did not know. I saw streets and squares which were strange to me.*[1] *Then I came into a house where I lived, went to my room, and found a letter from Mother lying there. She wrote saying that as I had left home without my parents' knowledge she had not wished to write to me to say that Father was ill. 'Now he is dead, and if you like*[2] *you can come.' I then went to the station ['Bahnhof'] and asked about a hundred times: 'Where is the station?' I always got the answer: 'Five minutes.' I then saw a thick wood before me which I went into, and there I asked a man whom I met. He said to me: 'Two and a half hours more.'*[3] *He offered to accompany me. But I refused and went alone. I saw the station in front of me and could not reach it. At the same time I had the usual feeling of anxiety that one has in dreams when one cannot move forward. Then I was at home. I must have been travelling in the meantime, but I know nothing about that. I walked into the porter's lodge, and inquired for our flat. The maidservant opened the door to me and replied that Mother and the others were already at the cemetery ['Friedhof'].*"[4]

It was not without some difficulty that the interpretation of this dream proceeded. In consequence of the peculiar circumstances in which the analysis was broken off—circumstances connected with the content of the dream—the whole of it was not cleared up. And for this reason, too, I am not equally certain at every point of the order in which my conclusions were reached. I will begin by mentioning the subject-matter with which the current analysis was dealing at the time when the dream intervened. For some time Dora herself had been raising a number of questions about the connection between some of her actions and the motives which presumably underlay them. One of these questions was: "Why did I say nothing about the scene by the lake for some days after it had happened?" Her second question was: "Why did I then sud-

---

[1] To this she subsequently made an important addendum: "*I saw a monument in one of the squares.*"

[2] To this came the addendum: "*There was a question-mark after this word, thus: 'like?'.*"

[3] In repeating the dream she said: "*Two hours.*"

[4] In the next sitting Dora brought me two addenda to this: "*I saw myself particularly distinctly going up the stairs,*" and "*After she had answered I went to my room, but not the least sadly, and began reading a big book that lay on my writing-table.*"

denly tell my parents about it?'' Moreover, her having felt so
deeply injured by Herr K.'s proposal seemed to me in general to
need explanation, especially as I was beginning to realize that Herr
K. himself had not regarded his proposal to Dora as a mere frivolous attempt at seduction. I looked upon her having told her parents
of the episode as an action which she had taken when she was
already under the influence of a morbid craving for revenge. A
normal girl, I am inclined to think, will deal with a situation of
this kind by herself. I shall thus present the material produced
during the analysis of this dream in the somewhat haphazard order
in which it recurs to my mind.

*She was wandering about alone in a strange town, and saw
streets and squares.* Dora assured me that it was certainly not
B——, which I had first hit upon, but a town in which she had
never been. It was natural to suggest that she might have seen
some pictures or photographs and have taken the dream-pictures
from them. After this remark of mine came the addendum about
the monument in one of the squares and immediately afterwards
her recognition of its source. At Christmas she had been sent an
album from a German health-resort, containing views of the town;
and the very day before the dream she had looked this up to show
it to some relatives who were stopping with them. It had been put
in a box for keeping pictures in, and she could not lay her hands
on it at once. She had therefore said to her mother: ''Where is the
box?''[5] One of the pictures was of a square with a monument in
it. The present had been sent to her by a young engineer, with
whom she had once had a passing acquaintance in the manufacturing town. The young man had accepted a post in Germany, so as
to become sooner self-supporting; and he took every opportunity
of reminding Dora of his existence. It was easy to guess that he
intended to come forward as a suitor one day, when his position
had improved. But that would take time, and it meant waiting.

The wandering about in a strange town was over-determined. It
led back to one of the exciting causes from the day before. A

---

[5] In the dream she said: *''Where is the station?''* The resemblance between the two
questions led me to make an inference which I shall go into presently.

young cousin of Dora's had come to stay with them for the holidays, and Dora had had to show him round Vienna. This cause was, it is true, a matter of complete indifference to her. But her cousin's visit reminded her of her own first brief visit to Dresden. On that occasion she had been a stranger and had wandered about, not failing, of course, to visit the famous picture gallery. Another cousin of hers, who was with them and knew Dresden, had wanted to act as a guide and take her round the gallery. *But she declined, and went alone,* and stopped in front of the pictures that appealed to her. She remained *two hours* in front of the Sistine Madonna, rapt in silent admiration. When I asked her what had pleased her so much about the picture she could find no clear answer to make. At last she said: "The Madonna."

There could be no doubt that these associations really belonged to the material concerned in forming the dream. They contained portions which reappeared in the dream unchanged ("she declined, and went alone" and "two hours"). I may remark at once that "pictures" was a point of junction in the network of her dream-thoughts (the pictures in the album, the pictures at Dresden). I should also like to single out, with a view to subsequent investigation, the theme of the "Madonna," of the virgin mother. But what was most evident was that in this first part of the dream she was identifying herself with a young man. This young man was wandering about in a strange place, he was striving to reach a goal, but he was being kept back, he needed patience and must wait. If in all this she had been thinking of the engineer, it would have been appropriate for the goal to have been the possession of a woman, of herself. But instead of this it was—a station. Nevertheless, the relation of the question in the dream to the question which had actually been put allows us to substitute *"box"* for "station."[6] A box and a woman: the notions begin to agree better.

She asked quite a hundred times. . . . This led to another exciting cause of the dream, and this time to one that was less indifferent. On the previous evening they had had company, and

---

[6] ["*Schachtel*," the word which was used for "box" by Dora in her question, is a depreciatory term for "woman."—*Trans.*]

afterwards her father had asked her to fetch him the brandy: he could not get to sleep unless he had taken some brandy. She had asked her mother for the key of the sideboard; but the latter had been deep in conversation, and had not answered her, until Dora had exclaimed with the exaggeration of impatience: "I've asked you *a hundred times* already where the key is." As a matter of fact, she had of course only repeated the question about *five times*.[7]

"Where is the *key*?" seems to me to be the masculine counterpart to the question "Where is the *box*?"[8] They are therefore questions referring to—the genitals.

Dora went on to say that during this same family gathering some one had toasted her father and had expressed the hope that he might continue to enjoy the best of health for many years to come, etc. At this a strange quiver had passed over her father's tired face, and she had understood what thoughts he was having to keep down. Poor sick man! Who could tell what span of life was still to be his?

This brings us to the *contents of the letter* in the dream. Her father was dead, and she had left home by her own choice. In connection with this letter I at once reminded Dora of the farewell letter which she had written to her parents or had at least composed for their benefit. This letter had been intended to give her father a fright, so that he should give up Frau K.; or at any rate to take revenge on him if he could not be induced to do that. We are here concerned with the subject of her death and of her father's death. (Cf. "cemetery" later on in the dream.) Shall we be going astray if we suppose that the situation which formed the facade of the dream was a phantasy of revenge directed against her father? The feelings of pity for him which she remembered from the day before would be quite in keeping with this. According to the phantasy she had left home and gone among strangers, and her father's heart had broken with grief and with longing for her. Then she would be revenged. She understood very clearly what it was that her father needed when he could

---

[7]In the dream the number five occurs in the mention of the period of "five minutes." In my book on the interpretation of dreams I have given several examples of the way in which numbers occurring in the dream-thoughts are treated by the dream. We frequently find them torn out of their true context and inserted into a new one.

[8]See the first dream, p. 58.

not get to sleep without a drink of brandy.[9] We will make a note of Dora's *craving for revenge* as a new element to be taken into account in any subsequent synthesis of her dream-thoughts.

But the contents of the letter must be capable of further determination. What was the source of the words "if you like"? It was at this point that the addendum of there having been a question-mark after the word "like" occurred to Dora, and she then recognized these words as a quotation out of the letter from Frau K. which had contained the invitation to L——, the place by the lake. In that letter there had been a question-mark placed, in a most unusual fashion, in the very middle of a sentence, after the intercalated words "if you would like to come."

So here we were back again at the scene by the lake and at the problems connected with it. I asked Dora to describe the scene to me in detail. At first she produced little that was new. Herr K.'s exordium had been somewhat serious; but she had not let him finish what he had to say. No sooner had she grasped the purport of his words than she had slapped him in the face and hurried away. I inquired what his actual words had been. Dora could only remember one of his pleas: "You know I get nothing out of my wife."[10] In order to avoid meeting him again she had wanted to get back to L—— on foot, by walking round the lake, and *she had asked a man whom she met how far it was*. On his replying that it was *"Two and a half hours,"* she had given up her intention and had after all gone back to the ship, which left soon afterwards. Herr K. had been there too, and had come up to her and begged her to forgive him and not to mention the incident. But she had made no reply.—Yes. The *wood* in the dream had been just like the wood by the shore of the lake, the wood in which the scene she had just described once more had taken place. But she had seen precisely the same thick wood the day before, in a picture at the Secessionist exhibition. In the background of the picture there were *nymphs*.[11]

---

[9]There can be no doubt that sexual satisfaction is the best soporific, just as sleeplessness is almost always the consequence of lack of satisfaction. Her father could not sleep because he was debarred from sexual intercourse with the woman he loved. (Compare in this connection the phrase discussed below: "I get nothing out of my wife.")

[10]These words will enable us to solve one of our problems.

[11]Here for the third time we come upon "picture" (views of towns, the Dresden gallery), but in a much more significant connection. Because of what appears in the

At this point a certain suspicion of mine became a certainty. The use of *"Bahnhof'* ["station"; literally, "railway-court"][12] and *"Friedhof'* ["cemetery"; literally, "peace-court"] to represent the female genitals was striking enough in itself, but it also served to direct my awakened curiosity to the similarly formed *"Vorhof'* ["vestibulum"; literally, "fore-court"]—an anatomical term for a particular region of the female genitals. This might have been no more than a misleading joke. But now, with the addition of "nymphs" visible in the background of a "thick wood," no further doubts could be entertained. Here was a symbolic geography of sex! "Nymphae,"[13] as is known to physicians though not to laymen (and even by the former the term is not very commonly used), is the name given to the labia minora, which lie in the background of the "thick wood" of the pubic hair. But any one who employed such technical names as "vestibulum" and "nymphae" must have derived his knowledge from books, and not from popular ones either, but from anatomical text-books or from an encyclopaedia—the common refuge of youth when it is devoured by sexual curiosity. If this interpretation were correct, therefore, there lay concealed behind the first situation in the dream a phantasy of defloration, the phantasy of a man seeking to force an entrance into the female genitals.[14]

I informed Dora of the conclusions I had reached. The impression made upon her must have been forcible, for there immediately appeared a piece of the dream which had been forgotten: *"she went calmly to her room, and began reading a big book that lay on her*

---

picture (the wood, the nymphs), the *"Bild"* ["picture"] is turned into a *"Weibsbild"* [literally, "picture of a woman"—a derogatory expression for "woman"].

[12]Moreover, a "station" is used for purposes of *"Verkehr"* ["traffic," "intercourse," "sexual intercourse"]: this affords the psychological wrapping in many cases of railway phobia.

[13][In German the same word, *"Nymphen,"* represents both "nymphs" and "nymphae."—*Trans.*]

[14]The phantasy of defloration formed the second component of the situation. The emphasis upon the difficulty of getting forward and the anxiety felt in the dream indicated the stress which the dreamer was so ready to lay upon her virginity—a point alluded to in another place by means of the Sistine Madonna. These sexual thoughts gave an unconscious ground-colouring to the wishes (which were perhaps merely kept secret) concerned with the suitor who was waiting for her in Germany. We have already recognized the phantasy of revenge as the first component of the same situation in the dream. The two components do not coincide completely, but only in part. We shall subsequently come upon the traces of a third and still more important train of thought.

writing-table."[15] The emphasis here was upon the two details "calmly" and "big" in connection with "book." I asked whether the book was in encyclopaedia *format,* and she said it was. Now children never read about forbidden subjects in an encyclopaedia *calmly.* They do it in fear and trembling, with an uneasy look over their shoulder to see if some one may not be coming. Parents are very much in the way while reading of this kind is going on. But this uncomfortable situation had been radically improved, thanks to the dream's power of fulfilling wishes. Dora's father was dead, and the others had already gone to the cemetery. She might calmly read whatever she chose. Did not this mean that one of her motives for revenge was a revolt against her parents' constraint? If her father was dead she could read or love as she pleased.

At first she would not remember ever having read anything in an encyclopaedia; but she then admitted that a recollection of an occasion of the kind did occur to her, though it was of an innocent enough nature. At the time when the aunt she was so fond of had been so seriously ill and it had already been settled that Dora was to go to Vienna, a *letter* had come from another uncle, to say that they could not go to Vienna, as a boy of his, a cousin of Dora's therefore, had fallen dangerously ill with appendicitis. Dora had thereupon looked up in the encyclopaedia to see what the symptoms of appendicitis were. From what she had then read she still recollected the characteristic localization of the abdominal pain.

I then remembered that shortly after her aunt's death Dora had had an attack of what had been alleged to be appendicitis. Up till then I had not ventured to count that illness among her hysterical productions. She told me that during the first few days she had had high fever and had felt the pain in her abdomen that she had read about in the encyclopaedia. She had been given cold

---

[15]On another occasion, instead of "calmly" she said "not the least sadly." (See footnote, p. 86)—I can quote this dream as fresh evidence for the correctness of an assertion which I made in my *Traumdeutung* (Seventh Edition, pp. 387 ff.) to the effect that those pieces of a dream which are at first forgotten and are only subsequently remembered are invariably the most important from the point of view of understanding the dream. In the same place I went on to the conclusion that the forgetting of dreams must also be explained as an effect of endopsychic resistance.

fomentations but had not been able to bear them. On the second day her period had set in, accompanied by violent pains. (Since her health had been bad, the periods had been very irregular.) At that time she used to suffer continually from constipation.

It was not really possible to regard this state as a purely hysterical one. Although hysterical fever does undoubtedly occur, yet it seemed too arbitrary to put down the fever accompanying this questionable illness to hysteria instead of to some organic cause operative at the time. I was on the point of abandoning the track, when she herself helped me along it by producing her last addendum to the dream: *"she saw herself particularly distinctly going up the stairs."*

I naturally required a special determinant for this. Dora objected that she would anyhow have had to go upstairs if she had wanted to get to her flat, which was on an upper floor. It was easy to brush aside this objection (which was probably not very seriously intended) by pointing out that if she had been able to travel in her dream from the unknown town to Vienna without making a railway journey she ought also to have been able to leave out a flight of stairs. She then proceeded to relate that after the appendicitis she had not been able to walk properly and had dragged her right foot. This state of things had continued for a long time, and on that account she had been particularly glad to avoid stairs. Even now her foot sometimes dragged. The doctors whom she had consulted at her father's desire had been very much astonished at this most unusual after-effect of an appendicitis, especially as the abdominal pains had not recurred and did not in any way accompany the dragging of the foot.[16]

Here, then, we have a true hysterical symptom. The fever may have been organically determined—perhaps by one of those very frequent attacks of influenza that are not localized in any particular part of the body. Nevertheless it was now established that the neurosis had seized upon this chance event and made use of it for an utterance

---

[16]We must assume the existence of some somatic connection between the painful abdominal sensations known as "ovarian neuralgia" and locomotor disturbances in the leg on the same side; and we must suppose that in Dora's case the somatic connection had been given an interpretation of a particularly specialized sort, that is to say, that it had been overlaid with and brought into the service of a particular psychological meaning. The reader is referred to my analogous remarks in connection with the analysis of Dora's symptom of coughing and with the relation between catarrh and anorexia.

of its own. Dora had therefore given herself an illness which she had read up about in the encyclopaedia, and she had punished herself for dipping into its pages. But she was forced to recognize that the punishment could not possibly apply to her reading the innocent article in question. It must have been inflicted as the result of a process of displacement, after another occasion of more guilty reading had become associated with this one; and the guilty occasion must lie concealed in her memory behind the contemporaneous innocent one.[17] It might still be possible, perhaps, to discover the nature of the subjects she had read about on that other occasion.

What, then, was the meaning of this condition, of this attempted simulation of a perityphlitis? The remainder of the disorder, the dragging of one leg, was entirely out of keeping with perityphlitis. It must, no doubt, fit in better with the secret and possibly sexual meaning of the clinical picture; and if it were elucidated might in its turn throw light upon the meaning which we were in search of. I looked about for a means of approaching the puzzle. Periods of time had been mentioned in the dream; and time is assuredly never a matter of indifference in any biological event. I therefore asked Dora when this attack of appendicitis had taken place; whether it had been before or after the scene by the lake. Every difficulty was resolved at a single blow by her prompt reply: "Nine months later." The period of time is sufficiently characteristic. Her supposed attack of appendicitis had thus enabled the patient with the modest means at her disposal (the pains and the menstrual flow) to realize a phantasy of *childbirth*.[18] Dora was naturally aware of the significance of this period of time, and could not dispute the probability of her having, on the occasion under discussion, read up in the encyclopaedia about pregnancy and childbirth. But what was all this about her dragging her leg? I could now hazard a guess. That is how people walk when they have twisted a foot. So she had made a "false step": which was true indeed if

---

[17]This is quite a typical example of the way in which symptoms arise from exciting causes which appear to be entirely unconnected with sexuality.

[18]I have already indicated that the majority of hysterical symptoms, when they have attained their full pitch of development, represent an imagined situation of sexual life— such as a scene of sexual intercourse, pregnancy, childbirth, confinement, etc.

she could give birth to a child nine months after the scene by the lake. But there was still another requirement upon the fulfilment of which I had to insist. I am convinced that a symptom of this kind can only arise where it has an *infantile* prototype. All my experience hitherto has led me to hold firmly to the view that recollections derived from the impressions of later years do not possess sufficient force to enable them to establish themselves as symptoms. I scarcely dared hope that Dora would provide me with the material that I wanted from her childhood, for the fact is that I am not yet in a position to assert the general validity of this rule, much as I should like to be able to do so. But in this case there came an immediate confirmation of it. Yes, said Dora, once when she was a child she had twisted the same foot; she had slipped on one of the steps as she was going *downstairs*. The foot—and it was actually the same one that she afterwards dragged—had swelled up and had to be bandaged and she had had to lie up for some weeks. This had been a short time before the attack of nervous asthma in her eighth year.

The next thing to do was to turn to account our knowledge of the existence of this phantasy: "If it is true that you were delivered of a child nine months after the scene by the lake, and that you are going about to this very day carrying the consequences of your false step with you, then it follows that in your unconscious you must have regretted the upshot of the scene. In your unconscious thoughts, that is to say, you have made an emendation in it. The assumption that underlies your phantasy of childbirth is that on that occasion something took place,[19] that on that occasion you experienced and went through everything that you were in fact obliged to pick up later on from the encyclopaedia. So you see that your love for Herr K. did not come to an end with the scene, but that (as I maintained) it has persisted down to the present day—though it is true that you are unconscious of it."—And Dora disputed the fact no longer.[20]

The labour of elucidating the second dream had so far occupied

---

[19]The phantasy of defloration is thus found to have an application to Herr K., and we begin to see why this part of the dream contained material taken from the scene by the lake—the refusal, two and a half hours, the wood, the invitation to L——.

[20]I may here add a few supplementary interpretations to those that have already been

two hours. At the end of the second sitting, when I expressed my satisfaction at the result, Dora replied in a depreciatory tone: "Why, has anything so very remarkable come out?" These words prepared me for the advent of fresh revelations.

She opened the third sitting with these words: "Do you know that I am here for the last time to-day?"—"How can I know, as you have said nothing to me about it?"—"Yes. I made up my mind to put up with it till the New Year.[21] But I shall wait no longer than that to be cured."—"You know that you are free to stop the treatment at any time. But for to-day we will go on with our work. When did

---

given: The *"Madonna"* was obviously Dora herself; in the first place because of the "adorer" who had sent her the pictures, in the second place because she had won Herr K.'s love chiefly by the motherliness she had shown towards his children, and lastly because she had had a child though she was still a girl (this being a direct allusion to the phantasy of childbirth). Moreover, the notion of the "Madonna" is a favourite counter-idea in the mind of girls who feel themselves oppressed by imputations of sexual guilt,—which was the case with Dora. A first suspicion of this connection came to me while I was working as a physician at the Psychiatric Clinic of the University. I there came across a case of confusional insanity with hallucinations, in which the attack, which ran a rapid course, turned out to be a reaction to a reproach made against the patient by her *fiancé*.—If the analysis had been continued, Dora's maternal longing for a child would probably have been revealed as an obscure though powerful motive in her behaviour.—The numerous questions which she had been raising latterly seem to have been belated derivatives of questions inspired by the sexual curiosity which she had tried to gratify with the encyclopaedia. The subjects which she read up in it were presumably pregnancy, childbirth, virginity, and so on.—In reproducing the dream Dora had forgotten one of the questions which need to be inserted into the course of the second situation in the dream. This question could only be: "Does Herr —— live here?" or "Where does Herr —— live?" There must have been some reason for her having forgotten this apparently innocent question, especially as she need not have brought it into the dream at all. This reason, it seems to me, lay in her surname itself, which also denoted an object and in fact more than one kind of object, and which could therefore be regarded as an "ambiguous" word. Unluckily I cannot give the name and show how well designed it was to indicate something "ambiguous" and "improper." This interpretation was supported by the discovery of a similar play upon words in another part of the dream, where the material was derived from Dora's recollections of her aunt's death ("they have already gone to the cemetery") and where there was similarly a play upon her aunt's name. These improper words seemed to point to a second and *oral* source of information, since the encyclopaedia would not cover them. I should not have been surprised to hear that this source had been Frau K. herself, Dora's calumniator. In that case she would have been the one person whom Dora generously spared, while she pursued the others with an almost malignant vindictiveness. Behind the almost limitless series of displacements which were thus brought to light, it was possible to divine the operation of a single simple factor—Dora's deep-rooted homosexual love for Frau K.

[21] It was December 31st.

you come to this decision?"—"A fortnight ago, I think."—"That sounds just like a maidservant or a governess—a fortnight's warning."—"There was a governess who gave warning with the K.'s, when I was on my visit to them that time at L——, by the lake."—"Really? You have never told me about her. Tell me."

"Well, there was a young girl in the house, who was the children's governess; and she behaved in the most extraordinary way to Herr K. She never said good morning to him, never answered his remarks, never handed him anything at table when he asked for it, and in short treated him like thin air. For that matter he was hardly any politer to her. A day or two before the scene by the lake, the girl took me aside and said she had something to tell me. She then told me that Herr K. had made advances to her at a time when his wife was away for several weeks; he had made violent love to her and had implored her to yield to his entreaties, saying that he got nothing from his wife, and so on."—"Why, those are the very words he used afterwards, when he made his proposal to you and you gave him the slap in his face."—"Yes. She had given way to him, but after a little while he had ceased to care for her, and since then she hated him."—"And this governess had given warning?"—"No. She meant to give warning. She told me that as soon as she felt she was thrown over she had told her parents what had happened. They were respectable people living in Germany somewhere. Her parents said that she must leave the house instantly; and, as she failed to do so, they wrote to her saying that they would have nothing more to do with her, and that she was never to come home again."—"And why had she not gone away?"—"She said she meant to wait a little longer, to see if there might not be some change in Herr K. She could not bear living like that any more, she said, and if she saw no change she should give warning and go away."—"And what became of the girl?"—"I only know that she went away."—"And she did not have a child as a result of the adventure?"—"No."

Here, therefore (and quite in accordance with the rules), was a piece of material information coming to light in the middle of the analysis and helping to solve problems which had previously been raised. I was able to say to Dora: "Now I know your motive for the slap in the face with which you answered Herr K.'s proposal. It was not that you were offended at his suggestions; you were actuated by jealousy and revenge. At the time when the governess was telling you her story you were still able to make use of your gift for putting on one side everything that is not agreeable to your feelings. But at the moment when Herr K. used the words "I get nothing out of my wife"—which were the same words he had used to the governess—fresh emotions were aroused in you and tipped the balance. 'Does he dare,' you said to yourself, 'to treat me like a governess, like a servant?' Wounded pride added to jealousy and to the conscious motives of common sense—it was too much.[22] To prove to you how deeply impressed you were by the governess's story, let me draw your attention to the repeated occasions upon which you have identified yourself with her both in your dream and in your conduct. You told your parents what happened—a fact which we have hitherto been unable to account for—just as the governess wrote and told *her* parents. You give me a fortnight's warning, just like a governess. The letter in the dream which gave you leave to go home is the counterpart of the governess's letter from her parents forbidding her to do so."

"Then why did I not tell my parents at once?"

"How much time did you allow to elapse?"

"The scene took place on the last day of June; I told my mother about it on July 14th."

"Again a fortnight, then—the time characteristic for a person in service. Now I can answer your question. You understood the poor girl very well. She did not want to go away at once, because she still had hopes, because she expected that Herr K.'s affections would return to her again. So that must have been your motive too. You waited for that length of time so as to see whether he would repeat his proposals; if he had, you would have concluded that he was in earnest, and did not mean to play with you as he had done with the governess."

"A few days after I had left he sent me a picture postcard."[23]

---

[22] It is not a matter of indifference, perhaps, that Dora may have heard her father make the same complaint about his wife, just as I myself did from his own lips. She was perfectly well aware of its meaning.

[23] Here is the point of contact with the engineer, who was concealed behind the figure of Dora herself in the first situation in the dream.

"Yes, but when after that nothing more came, you gave free rein to your feelings of revenge. I can even imagine that at that time you were still able to find room for a subsidiary intention, and thought that your accusation might be a means of inducing him to travel to the place where you were living."—"As he actually offered to do at first," Dora threw in.—"In that way your longing for him would have been appeased"—here she nodded assent, a thing which I had not expected—"and he might have made you the amends you desired."

"What amends?"

"The fact is, I am beginning to suspect that you took the affair with Herr K. much more seriously than you have been willing to admit so far. Had not the K.'s often talked of getting a divorce?"

"Yes, certainly. At first she did not want to, on account of the children. And now she wants to, but he no longer does."

"May you not have thought that he wanted to get divorced from his wife so as to marry you? And that now he no longer wants to because he has no one to replace her? It is true that two years ago you were very young. But you told me yourself that your mother was engaged at seventeen and then waited two years for her husband. A daughter usually takes her mother's love-story as her model. So you too wanted to wait for him, and you took it that he was only waiting till you were grown up enough to be his wife.[24] I imagine that this was a perfectly serious plan for the future in your eyes. You have not even got the right to assert that it was out of the question for Herr K. to have had any such intention; you have told me enough about him that points directly towards his having such an intention.[25] Nor does his behaviour at L—— contradict this view. After all, you did not let him finish his speech and do not know what he meant to say to you. Incidentally, the scheme would by no means have been so impracticable.

---

[24]The theme of waiting till the goal is reached occurs in the content of the first situation in the dream. I recognize in this phantasy of waiting for a fiancée a portion of the third component of that situation. I have already alluded to the existence of this third component.

[25]In particular there was a speech which he had made in presenting Dora with a letter-case for Christmas in the last year in which they lived together at B——.

Your father's relations with Frau K.—and it was probably only for this reason that you lent them your support for so long—made it certain that her consent to a divorce could be obtained; and you can get anything you like out of your father. Indeed, if your temptation at L—— had had a different upshot, this would have been the only possible solution for all the parties concerned. And I think that is why you regretted the actual event so deeply and emended it in the phantasy which made its appearance in the shape of the appendicitis. So it must have been a bitter piece of disillusionment for you when the effect of your charges against Herr K. was not that he renewed his proposals but that he replied instead with denials and slanders. You will agree that nothing makes you so angry as having it thought that you merely fancied the scene by the lake. I know now—and this is what you do not want to be reminded of—that you *did* fancy that Herr K.'s proposals were serious, and that he would not leave off until you had married him.''

Dora had listened to me without any of her usual contradictions. She seemed to be moved; she said good-bye to me very warmly, with the heartiest wishes for the New Year, and—came no more. Her father, who called on me two or three times afterwards, assured me that she would come back again, and said it was easy to see that she was eager for the treatment to continue. But it must be confessed that Dora's father was never entirely straightforward. He had given his support to the treatment so long as he could hope that I should "talk" Dora out of her belief that there was something more than a friendship between him and Frau K. His interest faded when he observed that it was not my intention to bring about that result. I knew Dora would not come back again. Her breaking off so unexpectedly, just when my hopes of a successful termination of the treatment were at their highest, and her thus bringing those hopes to nothing—this was an unmistakable act of vengeance on her part. Her purpose of self-injury also profited by this action. No one who, like me, conjures up the most evil of those half-tamed demons that inhabit the human breast, and seeks to wrestle with them, can expect to come through the struggle unscathed. Might I perhaps have kept the girl under my treatment if I myself had acted a part, if I had exaggerated the importance to me of her staying on, and had shown a warm personal interest in her—a course which, even after allowing for my position as her physician, would have been tantamount to providing her with a substitute for the affection she longed for? I do not know. Since in every case a part of the factors that are encountered under the form of resistance remains unknown, I have always avoided acting a part, and have contented myself with practising the humbler arts of psychology. In spite of every theoretical interest and of every endeavour to be of assistance as a physician, I keep the fact in mind that there must be some limits set to the extent to which psychological influence may be used, and I respect as one of these limits the patient's own will and understanding.

Nor do I know whether Herr K. would have done any better if it had been revealed to him that the slap Dora gave him by no means signified a final "No" on her part, but that it expressed the jealousy which had lately been roused in her, while her strongest feelings were still on his side. If he had disregarded that first "No," and had continued to press his suit with a passion which left room for no doubts, the result might very well have been a triumph of the girl's affection for him over all her internal difficulties. But I think she might just as well have been merely provoked into satisfying her craving for revenge upon him all the more thoroughly. It is never possible to calculate towards which side the decision will incline in such a conflict of motives: whether towards the removal of the repression or towards its reinforcement. Incapacity for meeting a *real* erotic demand is one of the most essential features of a neurosis. Neurotics are dominated by the opposition between reality and phantasy. If what they long for the most intensely in their phantasies is presented to them in reality, they none the less flee from it; and they abandon themselves to their phantasies the most readily where they need no longer fear to see them realized. Nevertheless, the barrier erected by repression can fall before the onslaught of a violent emotional excitement produced by a real cause; it is possible for a neurosis to be overcome by reality. But we have no general means of calculating through what person or what event such a cure can be effected.[26]

5. Postscript

It is true that I have introduced this paper as a fragment of an analysis; but the reader will have discovered that it is incomplete to a far greater degree than its title might have led him to expect. It is therefore only proper that I should attempt to give a reason for the omissions—which are by no means accidental.

A number of the results of the analysis have been omitted, because at the time when work was broken off they had either not been established with sufficient certainty or they required further study before any general statement could be made about them. At other points, where it seemed to be permissible, I have indicated

---

[26]I will add a few remarks upon the structure of this dream, though it is not possible to understand it thoroughly enough to allow of a synthesis being attempted. A prominent piece of the dream is to be seen in the phantasy of revenge against her father, which stands out like a façade in front of the rest. (She had gone away from home by her own choice; her father was ill, and then dead. . . . Then she went home; all the others were already at the cemetery. She went to her room, not the least sadly, and calmly began reading the encyclopaedia.) This part of the material also contained two allusions to her other act of revenge, which she had actually carried out, when she let her parents discover a farewell letter from her. (The letter—from her mother, in the dream—and the mention of the funeral of the aunt who had always been her model.)—Behind this phantasy lie concealed her thoughts of revenge against Herr K., for which she found an outlet in her behaviour to me. (The maidservant, the invitation, the wood, the two and a half hours—all these came from material connected with the events at L——.) Her recollection of the governess and of the latter's exchange of letters with her parents, is related, no less than her farewell letter, to the letter in the dream allowing her to come home. Her refusal to let herself be accompanied and her decision to go alone may perhaps be translated into these words: "Since you have treated me like a maidservant, I shall take no more notice of you, I shall go my own way by myself, and not marry."— Screened by these thoughts of revenge, glimpses can be caught in other places of material derived from tender phantasies based upon the love for Herr K. which still persisted unconsciously in Dora. ("I would have waited for you till I could be your wife"—defloration—childbirth.)—Finally, we can see the action of the fourth and most deeply buried group of thoughts—those relating to her love for Frau K.—in the fact that the phantasy of defloration is represented from the man's point of view (her identi- fication of herself with her admirer who lived abroad) and in the fact that in two places there are the clearest allusions to ambiguous speeches ("Does Herr —— live here?") and to that source of her sexual knowledge which had not been oral (the encyclopae- dia).—Cruel and sadistic tendencies find satisfaction in this dream.

the direction along which some particular solution would probably have been found to lie. I have in this paper entirely left out of account the technique, which does not at all follow as a matter of course, but by whose means alone the pure metal of valuable unconscious thoughts can be extracted from the raw material of the patient's associations. This brings with it the disadvantage of the reader being given no opportunity of testing the correctness of my procedure in the course of this exposition of the case. I found it quite impracticable, however, to deal simultaneously with the technique of analysis and with the internal structure of a case of hysteria: I could scarcely have accomplished such a task, and if I had, the result would have been almost unreadable. The technique of analysis demands an entirely separate exposition, which would have to be illustrated by numerous examples chosen from a very great variety of cases and which would not have to take the results obtained in each particular case into account. Nor have I attempted in this paper to substantiate the psychological postulates which will be seen to underlie my descriptions of mental phenomena. A cursory attempt to do so would have effected nothing; an exhaustive one would have been a volume in itself. I can only assure the reader that I approached the study of the phenomena revealed by observation of the psychoneuroses without being pledged to any particular psychological system, and that I then proceeded to adjust my views until they seemed adapted for giving an account of the collection of facts which had been observed. I take no pride in having avoided speculation; the material for my hypotheses was collected by the most extensive and laborious series of observations. The decidedness of my attitude on the subject of the unconscious is perhaps specially likely to cause offence, for I handle unconscious ideas, unconscious trains of thought, and unconscious emotional tendencies as though they were no less valid and unimpeachable psychological data than conscious ones. But of this I am certain—that any one who sets out to investigate the same region of phenomena and employs the same method will find himself compelled to take up the same position, however much philosophers may expostulate.

Some of my medical colleagues have looked upon my theory of hysteria as a purely psychological one, and have for that reason pronounced it *ipso facto* incapable of solving a pathological problem.

They will no doubt discover from this paper that their objection was based upon their having unjustifiably transferred what is a characteristic of the technique on to the theory itself. It is the therapeutic technique alone that is purely psychological; the theory does not by any means fail to point out that neuroses have an organic basis—though it is true that it does not look for that basis in any pathological-anatomical changes, and provisionally substitutes the conception of organic functions for the chemical changes which we should expect to find but which we are at present unable to apprehend. No one, probably, will be inclined to deny the sexual function the character of an organic factor, and it is the sexual function that I look upon as the foundation of hysteria and of the psychoneuroses in general. No theory of sexual life will, I suspect, be able to avoid assuming the existence of some definite sexual substances having an excitant action. Indeed, of all the clinical pictures which we meet with in clinical medicine, it is the phenomena of intoxication and abstinence in connection with the use of certain chronic poisons that most closely resemble the genuine psychoneuroses.

But, once again, in the present paper I have not gone fully into all that might be said to-day about "somatic compliance," about the infantile germs of perversion, about the erotogenic zones, and about our predisposition towards bisexuality; I have merely drawn attention to the points at which the analysis comes into contact with these organic bases of the symptoms. More than this could not be done with a single case. And I had the same reasons that I have already mentioned for wishing to avoid a cursory discussion of these factors. There is a rich opportunity here for further works, based upon the study of a large number of analyses.

Nevertheless, in publishing this paper, incomplete though it is, I had two objects in view. In the first place, I wished to supplement my book on the interpretation of dreams by showing how an art, which would otherwise be useless, can be turned to account for the discovery of the hidden and repressed parts of mental life. (Incidentally, in the process of analysing the two dreams dealt with in the paper, the technique of dream interpretation, which is similar to that of psychoanalysis, has come under consideration.) In the second place, I wished to stimulate interest in a whole group of phenomena of which science is still in complete ignorance to-day because they can only be brought to light by the use of this particular method. No one, I believe, can have had any true conception of the complexity of the psychological events in a case of hysteria—the juxtaposition of the most dissimilar tendencies, the mutual dependence of contrary ideas, the repressions and displacements, and so on. The emphasis laid by Janet upon the *"idée fixe"* which becomes transformed into a symptom amounts to no more than an extremely meagre attempt at schematization. Moreover, it is impossible to avoid the suspicion that, when the ideas attaching to certain excitations are incapable of becoming conscious, those excitations must act upon one another differently, run a different course, and manifest themselves differently from those other excitations which we describe as "normal" and which have ideas attaching to them of which we become conscious. When once things have been made clear up to this point, no obstacle can remain in the way of an understanding of a therapeutic method which removes neurotic symptoms by transforming ideas of the former kind into normal ones.

I was further anxious to show that sexuality does not simply intervene, like a *deus ex machina,* on one single occasion, at some point in the working of the processes which characterize hysteria, but that it provides the motive power for every single symptom, and for every single manifestation of a symptom. The symptoms of the disease are nothing else than *the patient's sexual activity.* A single case can never be capable of proving a theorem so general as this one; but I can only repeat over and over again—for I never find it otherwise—that sexuality is the key to the problem of the psychoneuroses and of the neuroses in general. No one who disdains the key will ever be able to unlock the door. I still await news of the investigations which are to make it possible to contradict this theorem or to limit its scope. What I have hitherto heard against it have been expressions of personal dislike or disbelief. To these it is enough to reply in the words of Charcot: "Ca n'empêche pas d'exister."

Nor is the case of whose history and treatment I have published a fragment in these pages well calculated to put the value of psychoanalytic therapy in its true light. Not only the briefness of the treatment (which hardly lasted three months), but another factor inherent in the nature of the case, prevented an improvement from being effected such as is attainable in other instances, where the improvement will be admitted by the patient and his relatives and will approximate more or less closely to a complete recovery. Satisfactory results of this kind are reached when the symptoms are maintained solely by the internal conflict between the tendencies concerned with sexuality. In such cases the patient's condition will be seen improving in proportion as he is helped towards a solution of his mental problems by the translation of pathogenic into normal material. The course of events is very different when the symptoms have become enlisted in the service of external motives, as had happened with Dora during the last two years. It is surprising, and might easily be misleading, to find that the patient's condition shows no noticeable alteration even though considerable progress has been made with the work of analysis. But in reality things are not as bad as they seem. It is true that the symptoms do not disappear while the work is proceeding; but they disappear a little while later, when the relations between patient and physician have been dissolved. The postponement of recovery or improvement is really only caused by the physician's own person.

I must go back a little, in order to make the matter intelligible. It may be safely said that during psychoanalytic treatment the formation of new symptoms is invariably stopped. But the productive powers of the neurosis are by no means extinguished; they are occupied in the creation of a special class of mental structures, for the most part unconscious, to which the name of *"transferences"* may be given.

What are transferences? They are new editions or facsimiles of the tendencies and phantasies which are aroused and made conscious during the progress of the analysis; but they have this peculiarity, which is characteristic for their species, that they replace some earlier person by the person of the physician. To put it another way: a whole series of psychological experiences are revived, not as belonging to the past, but as applying to the person of the physician at the present moment. Some of these transferences have a content which differs from that of their model in no respect whatever except for the substitution. These, then—to keep to the same metaphor—are merely new impressions or reprints.

Others are more ingeniously constructed; their content has been subjected to a moderating influence—to *sublimation,* as I call it—and they may even become conscious, by cleverly taking advantage of some real peculiarity in the physician's person or circumstances and attaching themselves to that. These, then, will no longer be new impressions, but revised editions.

If the theory of analytic technique is gone into, it becomes evident that transference is an inevitable necessity. Practical experience, at all events, shows conclusively that there is no means of avoiding it, and that this latest creation of the disease must be combated like all the earlier ones. This happens, however, to be by far the hardest part of the whole task. It is easy to learn how to interpret dreams, to extract from the patient's associations his unconscious thoughts and memories, and to practise similar explanatory arts: for these the patient himself will always provide the text. Transference is the one thing the presence of which has to be detected almost without assistance and with only the slightest clues to go upon, while at the same time the risk of making arbitrary inferences has to be avoided. Nevertheless, transference cannot be evaded, since use is made of it in setting up all the obstacles that make the material inaccessible to treatment, and since it is only after the transference has been resolved that a patient arrives at a sense of conviction of the validity of the connections which have been constructed during the analysis.

Some people may feel inclined to look upon it as a serious objection to a method which is in any case troublesome enough that it itself should multiply the labours of the physician by creating a new species of pathological mental products. They may even be tempted to infer from the existence of transferences that the patient will be injured by analytic treatment. Both these suppositions would be mistaken. The physician's labours are not multiplied by transference; it need make no difference to him whether he has to overcome any particular tendency of the patient's in connection with himself or with some one else. Nor does the treatment force upon the patient, in the shape of transference, any new task which he would not otherwise have performed. It is true that neuroses may be cured in institutions from which psychoanalytic treatment is excluded, that hysteria may be said to be cured not by the method but by the physician, and that there is usually a sort of blind dependence and a permanent bond between a patient and the physician who has removed his symptoms by hypnotic suggestion; but the scientific explanation of all these facts is to be found in the existence of "transferences" such as are regularly directed by patients on to their physicians. Psychoanalytic treatment does not create transferences, it merely brings them to light, like so many other hidden psychical factors. The only difference is this—that spontaneously a patient will only call up affectionate and friendly transferences to help towards his recovery; if they cannot be called up, he feels the physician is "antipathetic" to him, and breaks away from him as fast as possible and without having been influenced by him. In psychoanalysis, on the other hand, since the play of motives is different, all the patient's tendencies, including hostile ones, are aroused; they are then turned to account for the purposes of the analysis by being made conscious, and in this way the transference is constantly being destroyed. Transference, which seems ordained to be the greatest obstacle to psychoanalysis, becomes its most powerful ally, if its presence can be detected each time and explained to the patient.[1]

I have been obliged to speak of transference, for it is only by means of this factor that I can elucidate the peculiarities of Dora's analysis. Its great merit, namely, the unusual clarity which makes it seem so suitable as a first introductory publication, is closely bound up with its great defect, which led to its being broken off prematurely. I did not succeed in mastering the transference in good time. Owing to the readiness with which Dora put one part of the pathogenic material at my disposal during the treatment, I neglected the precaution of looking out for the first signs of transference, which was being prepared in connection with another part of the same material—a part of which I was in ignorance. At the beginning it was clear that I was replacing her father in her imagination, which was not unlikely, in view of the difference between our ages. She was even constantly comparing me with him consciously, and kept

---

[1] (*Additional Note*, 1923.)—A continuation of these remarks upon transference is contained in my technical essay upon "transference-love." ("Further Recommendations in the Technique of Psychoanalysis: Observations on Transference—Love," *Therapy and Technique*, Collier Books edition BS 189V.)

anxiously trying to make sure whether I was being quite straightforward with her, for her father "always preferred secrecy and roundabout ways." But when the first dream came, in which she gave herself the warning that she had better leave my treatment just as she had formerly left Herr K.'s house, I ought to have listened to the warning myself. "Now," I ought to have said to her, "it is from Herr K. that you have made a transference on to me. Have you noticed anything that leads you to suspect me of evil intentions similar (whether openly or in some sublimated form) to Herr K.'s? Or have you been struck by anything about me or got to know anything about me which has caught your fancy, as happened previously with Herr K.?" Her attention would then have been turned to some detail in our relations, or in my person or circumstances, behind which there lay concealed something analogous but immeasurably more important concerning Herr K. And when this transference had been cleared up, the analysis would have obtained access to new memories, dealing, probably, with actual events. But I was deaf to this first note of warning, thinking I had ample time before me, since no further stages of transference developed and the material for the analysis had not yet run dry. In this way the transference took me unawares, and, because of the unknown quantity in me which reminded Dora of Herr K., she took her revenge on me as she wanted to take her revenge on him, and deserted me as she believed herself to have been deceived and deserted by him. Thus she *acted* an essential part of her recollections and phantasies instead of reproducing it in the treatment. What this unknown quantity was I naturally cannot tell. I suspect that it had to do with money, or with jealousy of another patient who had kept up relations with my family after her recovery. When it is possible to work transferences into the analysis at an early stage, the course of the analysis is retarded and obscured, but its existence is better guaranteed against sudden and overwhelming resistances.

In Dora's second dream there are several clear allusions to transference. At the time she was telling me the dream I was still unaware (and did not learn until two days later) that we had only *two hours* more work before us. This was the same length of time which she had spent in front of the Sistine Madonna, and which (by making a correction and putting "two hours" instead of "two and a half hours'') she had taken as the length of the walk which she had not made around the lake. The striving and waiting in the dream, which related to the young man in Germany, and had their origin in her waiting till Herr K. could marry her, had been expressed in the transference a few days before. The treatment, she had thought, was too long for her; she would never have the patience to wait so long. And yet in the first few weeks she had had discernment enough to listen without making any such objections when I informed her that her complete recovery would require perhaps a year. Her refusing in the dream to be accompanied, and preferring to go alone, also originated from her visit to the gallery at Dresden, and I was myself to experience them on the appointed day. What they meant was, no doubt: "Men are all so detestable that I would rather not marry. This is my revenge."[2]

If cruel impulses and revengeful motives, which have already been used in the patient's ordinary life for maintaining her symptoms, become transferred on to the physician during treatment, before he has had time to detach them from himself by tracing them back to their sources, then it is not to be wondered at if the patient's condition is unaffected by his therapeutic efforts. For how could the patient take a more effective revenge than by demonstrating upon her own person the helplessness and incapacity of the physician? Nevertheless, I am not inclined to put too low a value upon the therapeutic results even of such a fragmentary treatment as Dora's.

---

[2] The longer the interval of time that separates me from the end of this analysis, the more probable it seems to me that the fault in my technique lay in this omission: I failed to discover in time and to inform the patient that her homosexual (gynaecophilic) love for Frau K. was the strongest unconscious current in her mental life. I ought to have guessed that the main source of her knowledge of sexual matters could have been no one but Frau K.—the very person who later on charged her with being interested in those same subjects. Her knowing all about such things and, at the same time, her always pretending not to know where her knowledge came from was really too remarkable. I ought to have attacked this riddle and looked for the motive of such an extraordinary piece of repression. If I had done this, the second dream would have given me my answer. The remorseless craving for revenge expressed in that dream was suited as nothing else to conceal the current of feeling that ran contrary to it—the magnanimity with which she forgave the treachery of the friend she loved and concealed from every one the fact that it was this friend who had herself revealed to her the knowledge which had later been the ground of the accusations against her. Before I had learnt the importance of the homosexual current of feeling in psychoneurotics, I was often brought to a standstill in the treatment of my cases or found myself in complete perplexity.

It was not until fifteen months after the case was over and this paper drafted that I had news of my patient's condition and the effects of my treatment. On a date which is not a matter of complete indifference, on the first of April (times and dates, as we know, were never without significance for her), Dora came to see me again: to finish her story and to ask for help once more. One glance at her face, however, was enough to tell me that she was not in earnest over her request. For four or five weeks after stopping the treatment she had been "all in a muddle," as she said. A great improvement had then set in; her attacks had become less frequent and her spirits had risen. In the May of that year one of the K.'s two children (it had always been delicate) had died. She took the opportunity of their loss to pay them a visit of condolence, and they received her as though nothing had happened in the last three years. She made it up with them, she took her revenge on them, and she brought her own business to a satisfactory conclusion. To the wife she said: "I know you have an affair with my father"; and the other did not deny it. From the husband she drew an admission of the scene by the lake which he had disputed, and brought the news of her vindication home to her father. Since then she had not resumed her relations with the family.

After this she had gone on quite well till the middle of October, when she had had another attack of aphonia which had lasted for six weeks. I was surprised at this news, and, on my asking her whether there had been any exciting cause, she told me that the attack had followed upon a violent fright. She had seen some one run over by a cart. Finally she came out with the fact that the accident had occurred to no less a person than Herr K. himself. She had come across him in the street one day; they had met in a place where there was a great deal of traffic; he had stopped in front of her as though in bewilderment, and in his abstraction he had allowed himself to be knocked down by a cart.[3] She had been able to convince herself, however, that he escaped without serious injury. She still felt some slight emotion if she heard any one speak of her father's affair with

---

[3] We have here an interesting contribution to the problem of indirect attempts at suicide, which I have discussed in my *Psychopathologie des Alltagslebens*.

Frau K., but otherwise she had no further concern with the matter. She was absorbed in her work, and had no thoughts of marrying.

She went on to tell me that she had come for help on account of a right-sided facial neuralgia, from which she was now suffering day and night. "How long has it been going on?" "Exactly a fortnight."[4] I could not help smiling; for I was able to show her that exactly a fortnight earlier she had read a piece of news that concerned me in the newspaper. (This was in 1902.) And this she confirmed.

Her alleged facial neuralgia was thus a self-punishment—remorse at having once given Herr K. a box on the ear, and at having transferred her feelings of revenge on to me. I do not know what kind of help she wanted from me, but I promised to forgive her for having deprived me of the satisfaction of affording her a far more radical cure for her troubles.

Years have again gone by since her visit. In the meantime the girl has married, and indeed—unless all the signs mislead me—she has married the young man who came into her associations at the beginning of the analysis of the second dream. Just as the first dream represented her turning away from the man she loved to her father—that is to say, her flight from life into disease—so the second dream announced that she was about to tear herself free from her father and had been reclaimed once more by the realities of life.

---

[4] For the significance of this period of time and its relation to the theme of revenge, see the analysis of the second dream.

II

Hysterical Phantasies and Their Relation to Bisexuality[1] (1908)

We are all familiar with the delusional phantasies of paranoiacs which portray the person's greatness or his sufferings, and occur in stereotyped forms with almost monotonous regularity. We also come across numerous accounts of the strange conditions under which certain perverts carry out their sexual gratification—either in imagination or in reality. Nevertheless, it may be new to some readers to hear that quite analogous mental productions are regularly present in all the psychoneuroses, particularly in hysteria, and that these so-called hysterical phantasies have important connections with the causes of the neurotic symptoms.

The common origin and normal prototype of all these phantastic creations are the so-called daydreams of adolescence, to which some, though perhaps inadequate, attention has been given in the literature on the subject.[2] They occur with perhaps equal frequency in both sexes; in girls and women they are invariably of an erotic nature, in men they may be either erotic or ambitious. The importance of the erotic factor in those of men should not, however, be under-estimated; a more precise investigation of the day-dreams of a man generally shows that all his heroic exploits, all his successes, are for

---

[1] First published in the *Zeitschrift für Sexualwissenschaft*, Bd. I., 1908; reprinted in *Sammlung*, Zweite Folge. [Translated by Douglas Bryan.]

[2] Cf. Breuer und Freud, *Studien über Hysterie*, 1895; Pierre Janet, *Névroses et idées fixes*, I., "Les rêveries subconscientes," 1898; Havelock Ellis, *Studies in the Psychology of Sex*, vol. i., "The Evolution of Modesty," 1904; Freud, *Die Traumdeutung*, 1900; A. Pick, *Über pathologische Träumerei und ihre Beziehungen zur Hysterie*, 1896.

the purpose of pleasing a woman, of being preferred by her to other men.[3] These phantasies are wish-fulfilments, products of frustration and desire; they are justly called day-dreams, for they give us the key to an understanding of night dreams, the nucleus of which is nothing else than these daytime phantasies, but complicated and distorted, and misunderstood by the conscious psychic system.[4]

These day-dreams are invested with great interest, carefully cherished and usually concealed with some shame, as though they belonged to the person's most intimate possessions. It is easy to recognize a day-dreamer in the street, however, by his sudden absent-minded smile, his way of talking to himself, or the hastening of his steps which marks the climax of the fancied situation. All hysterical attacks which I have been able to investigate up to the present have proved to be involuntary day-dreams of this kind breaking in upon ordinary life. Now our observations leave no room for doubt that phantasies of this sort may be unconscious as well as conscious in nature, and that as soon as they become unconscious they may become pathogenic, *i.e.*, may express themselves in symptoms or attacks. Under favourable circumstances consciousness may just be able to capture such an unconscious phantasy. After I had drawn the attention of one of my patients to her phantasies, she told me that on one occasion she had burst into tears in the street, and that, thinking quickly what she had been crying about, she realized the existence of a phantasy in her mind that a pianist well known in the town (but not personally acquainted with her) had entered into an intimate relationship with her, that she had had a child by him (she was childless), and that he had deserted her and her child and left them in misery. It was at this point of her romance that she burst into tears.

Unconscious phantasies have either always been unconscious and formed in the unconscious, or more often they were once conscious phantasies, day-dreams, and have been purposely forgotten and driven into the unconscious by "repression." Their content may then either have remained the same or may have been altered,

---

[3]Havelock Ellis is of the same opinion; *op. cit.*
[4]Cf. Freud, *Die Traumdeutung*, Dritte Auflage, p. 33 *et seq.*

so that the phantasies which are now unconscious are derivatives of phantasies that were once conscious. Now an unconscious phantasy has a very important connection with the sexual life of the person; it is actually identical with the phantasy which served the person in his sexual gratification during the period of masturbation. The masturbatory (in the widest sense, onanistic) act at that time consisted of two parts, one of which was the creation of the phantasy, and the other a manipulative performance for attaining auto-erotic gratification at the climax of the phantasy. It is known that these two components of the act have first had to be welded together.[5] Originally the active performance was a purely auto-erotic proceeding for the purpose of obtaining pleasure from a particular erotogenic part of the body. Later this performance became bound up with the idea of a wish emanating from the sphere of object-love, and served as a partial realization of the situation in which the phantasy culminated. If the person subsequently renounces this type of masturbatory gratification with phantasy, the action is given up, but the previously conscious phantasy becomes an unconscious one. It may happen that no other form of sexual gratification supervenes, the person remaining abstinent and not succeeding in sublimating his libido, that is, in deflecting his sexual excitation into higher channels; these are, then, the conditions under which the unconscious phantasy is re-stimulated, and under which it will grow and spread and, drawing upon the whole might of the person's need for love, will achieve expression of at least a part of its content in the form of a morbid symptom.

In this way such unconscious phantasies are the immediate precursors in the mind of a whole series of hysterical symptoms. The hysterical symptoms are nothing but the unconscious phantasies made manifest by "conversion," and in so far as the symptoms are of a somatic kind they are often enough drawn from within the range of the sexual feelings and motor innervations that originally accompanied the phantasy while it was still conscious. In this way the process of discontinuing masturbation is literally reproduced again backwards; while the final aim of the whole pathological process, restoration of

[5] Cf. Freud, *Drei Abhandlungen zur Sexualtheorie.*

the original primary sexual gratification, is achieved, though never, it is true, completely, yet always by a sort of approximation.

Those who study hysteria find their attention therefore very soon diverted from the symptoms and directed to the phantasies which give rise to the symptoms. The technique of psychoanalysis enables us first of all to infer the unconscious phantasies from the symptoms and then to enable the patient to become conscious of them. Now it has been found by this means that the content of the unconscious phantasies of hysterical patients is in complete accordance with the conscious ways in which perverts actually obtain gratification; and if any one requires examples of such situations he need only call to mind the world-famed orgies of the Roman Emperors, the madness of which, of course, was the product of the unrestrained power and liberty possessed by their creators. The delusions of paranoiacs are of a similar nature but are phantasies which achieve direct access to consciousness; they are based on the masochistic-sadistic component of the sexual instinct, and they too have their complete counterpart in certain unconscious phantasies of hysterical persons. Of practical importance, too, is the case of hysterical persons who may not express their phantasies as symptoms, but consciously realize them in action and thus imagine and actually bring about assaults, attacks, or sexual aggressions.

This method of psychoanalytic investigation, which proceeds from the conspicuous symptoms to the hidden unconscious phantasies, reveals everything that can be found out about the sexuality of psychoneurotics, including the fact which is the subject of this short preliminary publication.[6]

The reason why the relationship between the phantasies and the symptoms is no simple one but very complicated, is in all probability due to the obstacles which the unconscious phantasies meet with in seeking to find expression. As a rule, *i.e.* when the neurosis is fully developed and has persisted for some time, a particular symptom corresponds not to a single unconscious phantasy, but to

---

[6]The same is true of the relation between the "latent" dream-thoughts and the elements of the "manifest" dream content. See the section on dream-work in my *Traumdeutung*.

several such; and this correspondence, moreover, is no arbitrary one but obeys definite laws. At the beginning of the illness these complications are not likely to be all fully developed.

For the sake of general interest I will here trespass beyond the continuity of my argument and try to describe the nature of hysterical symptoms in a series of successively exhaustive formulas. They do not contradict one another, but they consist partly in attempts at greater completeness and more precise classification, and partly of applications of different points of view.

1. The hysterical symptom is the memory-symbol of the operation of certain (traumatic) impressions and experiences.

2. The hysterical symptom is a substitute, produced by "conversion," for the reactivation of these traumatic experiences by association.

3. The hysterical symptom is, like other mental products, the expression of a wish-fulfilment.

4. The hysterical symptom is a realization of an unconscious phantasy which serves as a wish-fulfilment.

5. The hysterical symptom serves the purposes of sexual gratification and represents a part of the sexual life of the person (corresponding to one of the components of his sexual instinct).

6. The hysterical symptom corresponds to the recurrence of a form of sexual gratification which was real in infantile life and has since been repressed.

7. The hysterical symptom arises as a compromise between two opposing affects or instinctual trends, of which one is attempting to express a partial impulse or component of the sexual constitution, while the other tries to suppress it.

8. The hysterical symptom may represent various unconscious non-sexual impulses, but can never dispense with a sexual significance.

Among these various definitions the seventh is the one which defines the hysterical symptom most completely as the realization of an unconscious phantasy, and the eighth recognizes the proper significance of the sexual factor. Some of the previous formulas lead up to this and are contained in it.

The connection between the symptoms and the phantasies makes it easy to arrive, by psychoanalysis of the former, at a knowledge of the components of the sexual instinct dominating the person concerned, which I have described in my *Drei Abhandlungen zur Sexualtheorie*. In some cases, however, investigation by this means yields an unsuspected result. It shows that for many symptoms it is not enough to resolve only one unconscious sexual phantasy or even a number of them, of which one, the most important and fundamental, is of a sexual nature; to resolve the symptom one has, on the contrary, to deal with two sexual phantasies, of which one has a masculine and the other a feminine character, so that one of these phantasies has its source in a homosexual trend. This new statement does not alter our seventh formula; an hysterical symptom must necessarily be a compromise between a libidinal and a repressing force, but incidentally it may represent a combination of two libidinal phantasies of an opposite sexual character.

I shall refrain from giving examples of this law. I have found from experience that short condensed analyses always fail in the convincing effect for which they are intended, and I must leave an account of fully analysed cases for another time.

I will, therefore, merely state the following formula and explain its import.

9. An hysterical symptom is the expression of both a masculine and a feminine unconscious sexual phantasy.

I must expressly mention that I cannot claim the same general validity for this formula as for the others. As far as I can see, it applies neither to all the symptoms of one case nor to all cases. On the contrary, it is not hard to find cases in which the antithetical sexual impulses have found expression in separate symptoms, so that the symptoms of the heterosexuality and the homosexuality can be as clearly distinguished from each other as the underlying latent phantasies. Nevertheless, the condition stated in this ninth formula is frequent enough, and important enough when it occurs to deserve particular emphasis. It seems to me to mark the highest degree of complexity in the way in which an hysterical symptom can be determined, and one may expect, therefore, to meet with it only when a neurosis has persisted for a long time and undergone considerable organization.[7]

The bisexual nature of hysterical symptoms can nevertheless be demonstrated in numerous cases, and this is in any event an interesting confirmation of my view that the assumption of a bisexual predisposition in man[8] is particularly clearly brought out by psychoanalysis of neurotics. A quite analogous condition occurs when anyone in his conscious masturbatory phantasies pictures himself both as the man and as the woman in an imagined situation; further counterparts of this are found in certain hysterical attacks in which the patient acts at one and the same time both parts of the underlying sexual phantasy—for instance, in one case I observed, the patient pressed her dress to her body with one hand (as the woman) while trying to tear it off with the other (as the man). These simultaneous contradictory actions largely obscure the situation which is otherwise so plastically portrayed in attacks, and thus serve very well to conceal the unconscious phantasy which is actually at work.

In treatment by psychoanalysis it is very important to be prepared for the bisexual meaning of a symptom. One need not then be surprised or misled if a symptom seems to persist with undiminished force though one of its sexual meanings has already been resolved. It is then still being maintained by the perhaps unsuspected opposite sexual trend. In the treatment of such cases one may also observe how the patient finds an easy way of *evading* analysis of one sexual meaning by diverting his associations constantly to the opposite meaning, as if along a parallel line.

---

[7]J. Sadger has recently discovered this independently in his own psychoanalyses, and even vouches for its general validity: *Die Bedeutung der psychoanalytischen Methode nach Freud.*

[8]*Drei Abhandlungen zur Sexualtheorie.*

III

General Remarks on
Hysterical Attacks[1] (1909)

A. When one psychoanalyses a patient subject to hysterical attacks one soon gains the conviction that these attacks are nothing but phantasies projected and translated into motor activity and represented in pantomime. It is true that these phantasies are unconscious but otherwise they are of the same nature as those that may be observed directly in day-dreams or revealed by an interpretation of nocturnal dreams. A dream frequently takes the place of an attack and still more frequently helps to explain one, since the same phantasy finds different forms of expression both in dreams and in attacks. One might expect by observing an attack to be able to discover the phantasy it represents, but this is rarely possible. As a rule the pantomimic representation of the phantasy undergoes distortions, due to the influence of the censorship, analogous to the hallucinatory ones of dreams, so that to begin with both these manifestations are rendered unintelligible either to the patient's conscious mind or to the observer's comprehension. An hysterical attack, therefore, must be subjected to the same analytic procedure as we use in dream-interpretation. Not only are the forces producing the distortion and the purpose of this distortion the same as those we are familiar with from the interpretation of dreams, but the technique of the distortion is the same also.

1. The attack becomes unintelligible through its representing several

---

[1]First published in the *Zeitschrift für Psychotherapie und medizinische Psychologie*, Bd. I., 1909; reprinted in *Sammlung*, Zweite Folge. [Translated by Douglas Bryan.]

phantasies simultaneously by means of the same material, that is, through *condensation*. Features common to two (or more) phantasies form the nucleus of the representation, as in dreams. The phantasies thus made to coincide are often of quite different kinds, for instance, a recent wish and the re-activation of an infantile impression; the same innervations are then made to serve both purposes, often most cleverly. Hysterical patients who make use of condensation to a considerable extent may find a single type of attack sufficient; others express a multiplicity of pathogenic phantasies by several types of attack.

2. The attack becomes obscured by the patient's undertaking the parts played by both the persons appearing in the phantasy, that is, through *multiple identification*. For instance, I have mentioned a case[2] in which a patient tore off her dress with one hand (as the man) while she pressed it to her body with the other (as the woman).

3. A particularly effective form of distortion is *antagonistic inversion of the innervation,* which is analogous to the very usual changing of an element into its opposite by dream-work. For instance, in an hysterical attack an embrace may be represented by the arms being drawn back convulsively until the hands meet above the spinal column. Possibly the well-known *arc de cercle* of major hysterical attacks is nothing but an energetic disavowal of this kind, by antagonistic innervation of the position suitable for sexual intercourse.

4. Scarcely less confusing and misleading is the *reversal of the sequence of events* in the phantasy, which again has its complete counterpart in some dreams which begin with the end of an action and finish with its beginning. For instance, an hysterical patient may have a phantasy of seduction, the content of which is that she is reading in a park, her dress being slightly raised so that one foot is visible; a gentleman approaches and speaks to her; they then go to some other place where a love-scene takes place. This phantasy may be acted in the attack in such a way as to begin with a convulsive stage corresponding to the act of intercourse; she may then get up, go to another room, sit down to read and reply to the imaginary remark made in accosting her.

The two last-mentioned forms of distortion give some indication

---

[2]"Hysterical Phantasies and Their Relation to Bisexuality," this volume, p. 113.

of the intensity of the resistance with which the repressed material has to deal, even when it breaks through in an hysterical attack.

B. The outbreak of hysterical attacks follows laws that are readily understood. Since the repressed complex consists of libidinal cathexis and ideational content (phantasy), the attack may be aroused (1) *associatively*, if the content of the complex (sufficiently charged) is stirred by a conscious occurrence; (2) *organically*, if from some internal somatic reasons or external influences on the mind the libidinal cathexis exceeds a certain amount; (3) in the service of the *primary tendency* (paranosic gain) as an expression of "flight into illness" if reality becomes painful or frightening, therefore as a *consolation;* (4) in the service of the *secondary tendencies* (epinosic gain) with which the state of illness becomes connected as soon as the patient can gain a useful purpose by the production of an attack. In the last case the attack is aimed at particular people; it may be put off until they are within reach, and gives an impression of conscious simulation.

C. Investigation of the childhood history of hysterical patients shows that the hysterical attack is a substitute for an *auto-erotic* gratification previously practised and since given up. In a great number of cases this gratification (masturbation by manipulation or pressure of the thighs, movement of the tongue, etc.) recurs during the attack itself during the deflection of consciousness. The outbreak of attacks due to an increase of libido and in the service of the primary tendency, as a consolation, then exactly repeats the conditions under which the patient at one time consciously employed this auto-gratification. The anamnesis of the patient then gives the following phases: (*a*) auto-erotic gratification without ideational content, (*b*) the same in connection with a phantasy which culminates in the act of gratification, (*c*) renunciation of the act with retention of the phantasy, (*d*) repression of this phantasy, which then breaks through in the hysterical attack either unchanged or else modified and adapted to new experiences, and (*e*) which may even restore the action producing gratification which belongs to the phantasy and has apparently been given up. This is a typical cycle of infantile sexual activity: repression, failure of the repression, and return of the repressed.

The involuntary passing of urine can certainly not be considered irreconcilable with the diagnosis of hysterical attacks; it merely repeats the infantile form of a violent pollution. Moreover, biting the tongue may be met with in undoubted cases of hysteria; it is no more inconsistent with hysteria than with love-making. It occurs in attacks more readily when the physician's questions have drawn the patient's attention to the difficulties of a differential diagnosis. Self-injury may occur in hysterical attacks (more frequently in the case of men) and then repeats an accident that happened during childhood (for instance, during a fight.)

The loss of consciousness, the *"absence"* of the hysterical attack, is derived from the fleeting but unmistakable loss of consciousness which can be observed at the climax of every intensive (also auto-erotic) sexual gratification. Where hysterical *"absences"* arise from pollutions in young female persons this development can be most clearly followed. The so-called hypnoidal states, *"absences"* during day-dreaming so frequent in hysterical cases, reveal the same origin. The mechanism of these *"absences"* is comparatively simple. In the first place all the attention is concentrated on the course of the process of gratification and this whole cathexis of attention is suddenly removed at the moment when gratification occurs, so that a momentary void in consciousness takes place. This gap in consciousness, which may be called a physiological one, is then extended in the service of repression until it takes up everything which the repressing faculty rejects.

D. It is that reflex mechanism of the coitus-action which we see becoming manifest during unrestrained surrender to a sexual activity and which is available to everybody, including women, that point the way to the motor discharge of the repressed libido in attacks. Even the ancients called coitus a "minor epilepsy." We may alter this statement: the hysterical fit is an equivalent of coitus. The analogy with the epileptic attack helps us little, since its genesis is even less intelligible to us than that of hysterical attacks.

In general, the hysterical attack, like every form of hysteria, in women recalls to action a form of sexual activity which existed during childhood, and had at that time a pronounced masculine character. One may often observe that it is just those girls who in the years before puberty showed a boyish character and inclinations who tend to become hysterical at puberty. In a whole series of cases the hysterical neurosis is nothing but an excessive overaccentuation of the typical wave of repression through which the masculine type of sexuality is removed and the woman emerges.[3]

---

[3]Cf. Freud, *Drei Abhandlungen zur Sexualtheorie.*